∞

The Happiness
of Heaven

F. J. Boudreaux, S.J.

The Happiness
of Heaven

And How to Attain the Joys
That Await You There

Distributed by:
ANGELUS PRESS
2918 Tracy Ave
Kansas City, MO 64109 USA
1-800-966-7337 • 1-816-753-3150

SOPHIA INSTITUTE PRESS®
Manchester, New Hampshire

The Happiness of Heaven: And How to Attain the Joys That Await You There was originally published without a subtitle in 1871 by John Murphy and Company, Baltimore, Maryland. This 1999 edition by Sophia Institute Press contains minor revisions to the original text.

Sophia Institute Press®
Box 5284, Manchester, NH 03108
1-800-888-9344
www.sophiainstitute.com

Imprimatur: Martin John, Archbishop of Baltimore

Library of Congress Cataloging-in-Publication Data

Boudreaux, F. J.
    The happiness of heaven : and how to attain the joys that await you there / F.J. Boudreaux.
        p.   cm.
    Originally published: Baltimore, Md. : J. Murphy and Co., 1871.
    Includes bibliographical references.
    ISBN 0-918477-95-6 (pbk. : alk. paper)
    1. Heaven — Christianity. 2. Catholic Church — Doctrines.
I. Title.
BT846.2.B66   1999
236'.24 — dc21   99-17442 CIP

99 00 01 02 03 10 9 8 7 6 5 4 3 2 1

Contents

Editor's Note: Unless otherwise noted, the biblical references in the following pages are based on the Douay-Rheims edition of the Old and New Testaments. Where applicable, quotations from the Douay-Rheims edition have been cross-referenced with the differing names and numeration in the Revised Standard Version, using the following symbol: (RSV =).

∞

The Happiness
of Heaven

Chapter One

∞

You will see God

Reason, Revelation, and the experience of six thousand years unite their voices in proclaiming that perfect happiness cannot be found in this world. It certainly cannot be found in creatures, for they were not clothed with the power to give it. It cannot be found even in the practice of virtue, for God has, in His wisdom, decreed that virtue should merit, but never enjoy, perfect happiness in this world. He has solemnly pledged Himself to give "eternal life"[1] to all who love and serve Him here on earth. He has promised a happiness so unspeakably great, that the apostle who "was caught up into Paradise"[2] and was favored with a glimpse thereof, tells us that mortal "eye hath not seen, nor ear heard, neither hath it entered into the heart of man, what things God hath prepared for them that love Him."[3]

This happiness — which is now so incomprehensible to us — is none other than the possession and enjoyment of God Himself in the Beatific Vision, as well as the perfect

[1] Cf. Matt. 19:29.
[2] Cf. 2 Cor. 12:4 (RSV = 2 Cor. 12:3).
[3] 1 Cor. 2:9.

The Happiness of Heaven

satisfaction of every rational craving of our nature in the glorious resurrection of the body. It is on this glorious happiness that we are going to meditate. First, we shall endeavor to obtain a definite idea of the Beatific Vision, which is the essential constituent of heavenly bliss.

∞

We envision Heaven in different ways

In meditating upon the happiness in store for the children of God, we are very apt to build up a heaven of our own, which naturally takes the shape and color which our sorrows, needs, and sufferings lend to it. The poor man, for instance, who has suffered much from toil and want, looks upon Heaven as a place of rest, abounding with all that can satisfy the cravings of nature. Another, who has often endured the pangs of disease, looks upon it as a place where he shall enjoy perpetual health of body and mind. Another again, who, in the practice of virtue, has had all manner of temptations from the Devil, the world, and his own flesh, delights in viewing Heaven as a place totally free from temptation, where the danger, or even the possibility, of sin shall be no more.

All these, and other similar views of Heaven, are true inasmuch as they represent it as a place entirely free from evil and suffering, and, at the same time, as an abode of positive happiness. Nevertheless, they are all imperfect views, because not one of them takes in the whole of heavenly bliss, such as God has revealed it to us. They all ignore the Beatific Vision, which is the essential happiness of Heaven.

But even among those who look upon Heaven as a place where we still see God, very few indeed understand what is implied in the vision of God. Many imagine that we shall simply gaze upon an object whose surpassing perfection will make us happy in a way that we do not understand. These do not fully comprehend what is meant by the Beatific Vision, although they view Heaven as a place where we shall see God.

Let us, therefore, endeavor to understand what Faith and theology teach us concerning the Beatific Vision. We shall see that it is the essential happiness of the blessed, which fills them with the purest and most complete satisfaction, and, moreover, that it is in virtue of this Beatific Vision that the blessed are enabled to enjoy the additional or secondary pleasures which cluster around the throne of God.

∽

The two types of happiness in Heaven

Theologians divide the happiness of Heaven into *essential* and *accidental*. By *essential* is meant the happiness which the soul receives immediately from God in the Beatific Vision. By *accidental* is meant the additional pleasures or joys which come to the blessed from creatures.

Therefore, when our blessed Lord says, "There shall be joy in Heaven upon one sinner doing penance,"[4] He evidently means a new joy, which the blessed did not possess until sorrow for sin entered that sinner's heart. They were already happy in the Beatific Vision and would not have lost the slightest degree of their blessedness, even if that sinner had never repented of his sins. Still, they experience a new joy in his conversion, because in it they see God glorified; moreover,

[4] Luke 15:7.

they have reason to look for an additional brother or sister to share their bliss.

Yet, although the blessed do rejoice in the conversion of the sinner, they do so in virtue of the Beatific Vision — without which they could receive no additional pleasure from creatures. Therefore, the Beatific Vision is not only the essential happiness of Heaven, but it is also that which imparts to the saints the power of appropriating all the other inferior joys with which God completes the blessedness of His children. As this is a point of importance, we shall endeavor to understand it more clearly by an illustration.

A man who is gifted with perfect health of body and mind not only enjoys life itself, but he likewise receives pleasure from the beauties of nature — from literature, amusements, and society. Now, suppose he loses his health and is thrown on a bed of sickness. He is no longer able to enjoy either life itself or its pleasures. What is all the beauty of earthly or heavenly objects to him now? What are amusements, and all the joys of sense, which formerly delighted him so much? All these things are now unable to give him any pleasure, because he has lost his health, which afforded him the power of appropriating the pleasures of life. Therefore, we say that health is essentially necessary, not only to enjoy life itself, but also to relish its pleasures.

So, too, is it in Heaven. The Beatific Vision is necessary not only to enjoy the very life of Heaven, but likewise to enjoy the accidental glory with which God perfects the happiness of His elect.

What, then, is this Beatific Vision? Is it an eternal gazing upon God? Is it an uninterrupted "Ah!" of admiration? Or is it a sight of such overpowering grandeur as to deprive us of consciousness and throw us into a state of dreamy inactivity? We shall see.

∞

The meaning of the Beatific Vision

"Beatific Vision" is composed of three Latin words: *beatus*, happy; *facio*, I make; and *visio*, a sight — all of which, taken together, make up and mean a happy-making sight. Therefore, in its very etymology, Beatific Vision means a sight which contains in itself the power of banishing all pain and all sorrow from the beholder, and of infusing, in their stead, joy and happiness.

We shall now analyze this Beatific Vision and see wherein it consists.

Theologians tell us that the Beatific Vision, considered as a perfect and permanent state, consists of three acts, which are essential to its integrity and perfection: the sight, or vision, of God; the love of God; and the enjoyment of God. These three acts, although really distinct from each other, are inseparable, for, if even one of them is excluded, the Beatific Vision no longer exists in its integrity.

We shall now say a few words on each of these constituents of heavenly bliss.

∞

The sight of God

The sight, or vision, of God means that the intellect, which is the noblest faculty of the soul, is suddenly elevated by the light of glory and enabled to see God as He is, by a clear and unclouded perception of His Divine Essence. It is, thus, a vision in which the soul sees God, face-to-face — not indeed with the eyes of the body, but with the intellect. For God is a spirit and cannot be seen with material eyes. If our bodily eyes were necessary for that vision, we would not be able to see God until the day of judgment, for it is only then that our eyes will be restored to us. Hence, it is the soul that sees God, but when it does, the soul sees Him more clearly and perfectly than we can now see anything with our material eyes.

This vision of God is an intellectual act by which the soul is filled to overflowing with an intuitive knowledge of God — a knowledge so perfect and complete that all the knowledge of Him attainable in this world by prayer and study is like the feeble glimmer of the lamp compared with the dazzling splendor of the noonday sun.

This perfect vision, or knowledge, of God, is not only the first essential element of the Beatific Vision, but it is, moreover, the very root or fountainhead of the other acts which are necessary for its completeness. Thus we say of the sun that it is the source of the light, heat, life, and beauty of this material world, for, if the sun were blotted out from the heavens, this now beautiful world would, in one instant, become the dark and silent grave of every living creature. This is only a faint image of the darkness and sadness which would seize upon the blessed, if we could suppose that God would at any time withdraw from them the clear and unclouded vision of Himself. We say, therefore, that the vision of the Divine Essence is the root or source of the Beatific Vision.

Yet, although this is true, it does not follow that the vision of the Divine Essence constitutes the whole Beatific Vision, for the human mind cannot rest satisfied with knowledge alone, however perfect it may be. It must also love and enjoy the object of its knowledge. Therefore, the vision of God produces the two other acts which we shall now briefly consider.

∞

The love of God

The second element of the Beatific Vision is an act of perfect and inexpressible love. It is the sight or knowledge of God as He is that produces this love, because it is impossible for the soul to see God in His divine beauty, goodness, and unspeakable love for the soul without loving Him with all the power of its being. It would be easier to go near an immense fire and not feel the heat, than to see God in His very essence and yet not be set on fire with divine love.

It is, therefore, a necessary act — that is, one which the blessed could not possibly withhold, as we now can in this world. For, with our imperfect vision of God, as He is reflected from the mirror of creation, we can, and unfortunately do, withhold our love from Him — even when the light of faith is superadded to the knowledge we might have of Him from the teachings of nature. This is not so in Heaven. There, the blessed see God as He is, and therefore, they love Him spontaneously, intensely, and supremely.

∞

The enjoyment of God

The third element of the Beatific Vision is an act of excessive joy, which proceeds spontaneously from both the vision and the love of God. It is an act by which the soul rejoices in the possession of God, who is the Supreme Good. He is the soul's own God, the soul's own possession, and in the enjoyment of Him, the soul's cravings for happiness are completely gratified. Evidently, then, the Beatific Vision necessarily includes the possession of God, because without it, this last act could have no existence, and the true happiness of the blessed would not be complete, if we could suppose it to exist at all. A moment's reflection will make this as evident as the light of day.

A beggar, for instance, gazes upon a magnificent palace, filled with untold wealth, and all that can gratify the senses. Does the mere sight of it make him happy? It certainly does not, because it is not and never can be his. He may admire its grand architecture and exquisite workmanship and thus receive some trifling pleasure; but, as he can never call that palace nor its wealth his own, the mere gazing upon it, and even loving its beauty, can never render him happy. For this, the possession of it is essential.

Again, the starving beggar gazes upon the rich man's table loaded with every imaginable luxury. Does that mere sight relieve the pangs of hunger? It certainly does not. It rather adds to his wretchedness by intensifying his hunger without satisfying its cravings. So it would be in Heaven, if we could imagine a soul admitted there and allowed to gaze upon the beauty of God, while not able to possess or enjoy Him. Such a sight would be no Beatific Vision for that soul.

The possession of God is, therefore, absolutely necessary in order that the soul may enjoy Him and rest in Him as its last end. Hence, the act of seeing God is also the act by which the blessed possess God and enter into the joy of their Lord.

∞

The blessed participate in the divine nature
But this is not yet all. We have been considering the acts by which the soul appropriates God to itself, but we must not forget that the active concurrence of God is as essential in the Beatific Vision as is the action of the creature. The Beatific Vision means, therefore, that God not only enables the soul to see Him in all His surpassing beauty, but also takes the soul to His bosom as a beloved child and bestows upon it the happiness which mortal eyes cannot see. It means, furthermore, that God unites the soul to Himself in so wonderful and intimate a manner, that, without losing its created nature or personal identity, the soul is transformed into God, according to the forcible expression of St. Peter, when he asserts that we are "made partakers of the divine nature."[5] This is the highest glory to which a rational nature can be elevated, if we except the glory of the Hypostatic Union[6] and the maternity of the Blessed Virgin Mary.

In explaining this partaking of the divine nature in Heaven, theologians make use of a very apt comparison. If, they say, you thrust a piece of iron into the fire, it soon loses its dark color and becomes red and hot, like the fire. It is thus made a partaker of the nature of fire, without, however, losing its own essential iron nature. This illustrates what takes place in the Beatific Vision in relation to the soul. It is united to God and penetrated by Him. It becomes bright with His brightness,

---

[5] 2 Pet. 1:4.

[6] The Hypostatic Union refers to the union of the divine and human natures in the person of Christ.

beautiful with His beauty, pure with His purity, happy with His unutterable happiness, and perfect with His divine perfections. In a word, it becomes a partaker of the "divine nature," while it retains its created nature and personal identity.

Abstract words and reasoning, however, fail to convey a definite idea of this glorious happiness reserved for the children of God. Let us, therefore, have recourse to an illustration in the shape of a little parable. It will be as a mirror, wherein we shall see faint but true reflections of the Beatific Vision.

A kind-hearted king, while hunting in a forest, finds a blind orphan boy, totally destitute of all that can make life comfortable. The king, moved with compassion, takes him to his palace, adopts him as his own, and orders him to be cared for and educated in all that a blind person can learn. It is almost needless to say that the boy is unspeakably grateful and does all he can to please the king. When he has reached his twentieth year, a surgeon performs an operation upon his eyes, by which his sight is restored. Then the king, surrounded by his nobles and amid all the pomp and magnificence of the court, proclaims him one of his sons and commands all to honor and love him as such. And thus, the once-friendless orphan becomes a prince and, therefore, a partaker of the royal dignity, of the happiness and glory which are to be found in the palaces of kings.

I will not attempt to describe the joys that overwhelm the soul of this fortunate young man when he first sees that king, of whose manly beauty, goodness, power, and magnificence he had heard so much. Nor will I attempt to describe those other joys which fill his soul when he beholds himself, his own personal beauty, and the magnificence of his princely garments, of which he had also heard so much. Much less will I attempt to picture his exquisite and unspeakable happiness when he sees himself adopted into the royal family, honored and loved by all, together with all the pleasures of life within his reach. Each one may endeavor to imagine his feelings, joy, and happiness. We can only say that all this taken together is a beatific vision for him — in the natural order.

Here we find the three acts already explained. The first is the sight of the good king in all his glory and magnificence; the second is the intense love which this sight produces; and the third is the enjoyment of the king's society and all the happiness with which his adoption has surrounded him.

∞

God prepares you for Heaven

The application of the parable is obvious. God is the great and mighty King who finds your soul in the wilderness of this world. To use the forcible words of Scripture, He found you "wretched, and miserable, and poor, and blind, and naked."[7] Moved with compassion, He brought you into His holy Church. There, He washed you with His own Precious Blood, clothed you with the spotless robe of innocence, adorned you with the gifts of grace, and adopted you as His own child. Then He commanded His ministers and others to educate you for Heaven. By His grace, and your own cooperation, your soul is being gradually developed into a more perfect resemblance to Jesus Christ, who, in His human nature, is the standard of all created perfection.

[7] Rev. 3:17.

But you are blind yet, and must remain so until your heavenly Father calls you home. When that happy day dawns, you will leave this world, your eyes will be opened by the light of glory, and you will see God as He is, in all His glory and magnificence. You will see yourself as you are, adorned with the jewels of the many graces He has bestowed upon you. You will also see the beautiful angels and saints, clothed with the beauty of God Himself, standing around His throne to hear the sentence that will admit you into their society.

This sight of the living God, and of all the magnificence which surrounds Him, will fill your soul with a perfect knowledge of Him; and this knowledge will produce a most ardent and perfect love. And when He presses you to His bosom, proclaims you one of His children, and commands all to honor and love you as such, your joy will be full. This will be emphatically a Beatific Vision for you. You will then enter into the possession and enjoyment of God, who alone can fill the soul with pure and permanent happiness.

We shall now close this chapter with a beautiful extract from the great theologian Lessius. Speaking of the three acts which constitute the Beatific Vision, he says, "In these three acts resides God's chiefest glory, which He Himself intended in all His works; and so, likewise, in these same acts reside the highest good and formal beatitude of men and angels.

"By these acts the blessed spirits are vastly elevated above themselves, and, in their union with God, become godlike, by a most lofty and supereminent similitude with God, so that the mind can conceive no greater. Thus, like very gods, they shine to all eternity in the divine brightness. By these same acts, they expand themselves into immensity, so as to be co-equal and co-extensive, as far as may be, to so great a good, that they may take it in and comprehend it all. They linger not outside, as it were, upon the surface of it; but they go down into its profound depths and enter into the joy of their Lord; some more, some less, according to the magnitude of the light of glory imparted to each. Immersed in this abyss, they lose themselves and all created things, for all other good and joys seem to them as nothing by the side of this ocean of good and joys.

"In this abyss there is to them no darkness, no obscurity, such as now hangs over us about the Divinity, but all is light and immense serenity. There are their eternal mansions, with a tranquil security that they can never fail. There is the fulfilling of all their desires. There is the possession and enjoyment of all things that are desirable. There nothing will remain to be longed for or sought for anymore, for all will firmly possess and exquisitely enjoy every good thing in God.

"There the occupation of the saints will be to contemplate the infinite beauty of God, to love His infinite goodness, to enjoy His infinite sweetness, to be filled to overflowing with the torrent of His pleasures, and to exult with an unspeakable delight in His infinite glory, and in all the good things which He and they possess. Hence come perpetual praise, and benediction, and thanksgiving; and thus the blessed, having reached the consummation of all their desires, and knowing not what more to crave, rest in God as their last end."[8]

---

[8] Leonhard Lessius (1554-1623; Jesuit theologian), *On Divine Perfection*, Bk. 14, ch. 5.

Chapter Two

∞

God will perfect your soul

In the Beatific Vision, "we shall be like Him, because we shall see Him as He is."[9]

In the preceding chapter, we endeavored to understand the meaning of the Beatific Vision. We have seen that it is not a mere gazing upon God, but a true possession and enjoyment of Him. We have seen, moreover, that the Beatific Vision implies a most intimate union with God, in which the soul is made a partaker of the divine nature, in a far higher degree than is attainable in this world.

But we must be careful not to confuse this union of the soul with God — which is a moral union — with a personal union, such as exists between the humanity and the divinity in Jesus Christ. For, in Him, although these two natures are distinct, they are inseparable. Christ's human nature is so intimately united to the divine, that it receives its personality from the eternal Son of God. Hence, we cannot say that Jesus Christ is one person as man and another person as God, thus asserting two distinct persons in Christ. This would be a heresy, long since condemned by the Church. In Him, therefore, there is

[9] 1 John 3:2.

but one person, and that person is the eternal Son of God, in whom the human nature has not a distinct personality of its own. This is called a personal union or Hypostatic Union, which belongs to Jesus Christ alone and constitutes Him the Lord of lords, the King of kings, and the Judge of the living and the dead. No other creature, not even the Blessed Virgin, can ever aspire to such a union with God.

When, therefore, we speak of our intimate union with God in the Beatific Vision, we understand a moral union, and not a physical or a personal one. Hence, however intimate our union with God may be, we shall always retain our personality and never be merged into God.

In this world, however intimate the union which exists between friend and friend, parent and child, or husband and wife may be, these persons all retain their respective personalities. So shall it be in Heaven. We shall see and possess God; we shall be united to Him in an intimate manner, but we shall ever retain our distinct personality and individuality. When a drop of water falls into the ocean, it is absorbed and completely lost in that immense volume of water. This is no paradigm of our union with God. But the drop of oil is such a paradigm, for while it floats on the bosom of the deep, it does not mingle with the water, nor lose its individuality. It remains a drop of oil.

∽

God will perfect you

Not only shall we thus retain our personality when united to God in the Beatific Vision, but we shall, moreover, retain all that belongs to the reality of human nature. For, as St.

God will perfect your soul

Thomas teaches, "the glory of Heaven does not destroy nature, but perfects it."[10] Therefore, when Scripture tells us that
"we shall be changed,"[11] we must not imagine that we shall be
changed into angels, or into some other nature different from
the human. The change means a supernatural elevation and
perfection of our whole nature, and not its destruction. The
transition, or change, of the child into the man neither changes
nor destroys the faculties of his mind or the senses of his body;
nor does it create new powers or faculties which he had not before. His gradual growth into manhood only develops and perfects what the hand of God had placed in his nature on the day
of his creation.

This gradual development of our nature to its perfection,
in the natural order, illustrates the wonderful supernatural
perfection which the power of God will work in us in both the
Beatific Vision and the glorious resurrection of the body. For,
however great and elevated we may then be, our now existing
natural powers will neither be changed nor destroyed.

I have been thus careful in explaining these things, because
we are now to study the transforming power of the Beatific Vision upon the soul, as well as the glory of the spiritualized body
in which we shall again be clothed on the resurrection day.

According to the Angelic Doctor, the human soul bears a
threefold resemblance to God. It is like God by nature, by
grace, and by glory.[12] The likeness to God by nature is found in

[10] St. Thomas Aquinas (c. 1225-1274; Dominican philosopher
and theologian), *Summa Theologica*, I, Q. 62, art. 7.
[11] 1 Cor. 15:52.
[12] *Summa Theologica*, I, Q. 93, art. 4.

all men, but is imperfect. The likeness by grace is far more perfect; it is found in the just only, and it is seen in its full perfection in the blessed. We shall, therefore, endeavor to fathom
the meaning of St. John when he says, "We shall be like Him:
because we shall see Him as He is," as well as the saying of St.
Peter, who asserts that we shall be "made partakers of the divine nature."[13] Let us begin by a little illustration.

Suppose you enter an artist's studio, just as he has drawn
the outlines of a portrait. All the essential features are there —
the shape of the head, the eyes, ears, mouth, and whatever else
is necessary to constitute the human face — and it already
bears a striking resemblance to the man who is sitting for his
portrait. You return in a few days, and, although the portrait is
yet far from being finished, the coloring has added so much
that it is far more beautiful and perfect than when you first saw
it. Again, you see it when it is completely finished, framed,
and exposed to public view. How perfect! How lifelike it is! It
actually seems to live and breathe. How vast a difference between this exquisitely finished painting and the mere outlines
you first saw! This illustration teaches us, better than abstract
words could do, how the human soul is like God from the very
first, and how that likeness gradually increases by grace and
the practice of virtue, until it receives the last touch and finish
in the Beatific Vision.

From the very first moment of its existence, the soul is like
God, because it is a spirit and therefore immortal. It is endowed with intelligence, free will, memory, and whatever else
belongs to a spiritual substance. Evidently, this is already the

---

[13] 2 Pet. 1:4.

image of God, although, compared with what it will be by grace and the Beatific Vision, it is as yet nothing more than the mere outlines.

Next comes Baptism, by which the soul is raised to the supernatural state. It is washed with the blood of Jesus and clothed with the robe of innocence, which, if we may use the expression, begins the coloring or beautifying process. Faith, hope, and charity are infused into the soul, which enables it to lead a supernatural life. Then come other sacraments, whose purpose is to wash away stains, to remove imperfections, and to nourish, strengthen, beautify, and gradually develop a greater resemblance to God.

∞

God calls for your cooperation

But there is an immense difference between the senseless image we saw on the canvas and the soul. The portrait is a lifeless image, which is totally passive, and has, therefore, nothing whatever to do with its gradual growth and its resemblance to the original. It is not so with the soul. It is a living and rational image of the eternal God and has the power to aid very materially in its gradual development and in its greater resemblance to the original, which is God. It has not only the power, but also the strict obligation of cooperating with God in perfecting what He began without its cooperation.

Hence, while of itself the soul is incapable of having even a good thought, aided by the grace of God it has not only good thoughts and desires, but also the strength to carry them into effect. With God's assistance, it can and does reproduce in itself the virtues which Jesus taught and practiced — His humility, purity, meekness, obedience, patience, and resignation to God's will. Especially does it reproduce His life of love — love for God and love for man.

As soon as this divine charity becomes the mainspring of its actions, everything the soul does develops in it a greater resemblance to God. Then, not only prayer, the sacraments, spiritual reading, and other spiritual exercises, but also voluntary mortifications, temptations from the Devil, the world, and the flesh — even eating, drinking, and innocent recreations — all help powerfully to develop and perfect in the soul the image of God. For, as St. Paul tells us, "To them that love God, all things work together unto good."[14]

If you could now see a soul at the first moment of its existence, you would see the image of God begun. If you could see the soul again immediately after Baptism, it would appear far more beautiful, because it would then be clothed with the robe of innocence and beautified by the grace of God. But if you could see that same soul after ten, twenty, or more years of a holy life, you would scarcely believe that it was the same soul, so much more God-like and beautiful would it have become. But again, if you could see the soul united to God in the Beatific Vision, you would be so overpowered with its dazzling splendor and unearthly beauty, that you would be ready to fall down and adore it — thinking that it was God Himself you were seeing and not His image. The soul would have to prevent this adoration, by assuring you that whatever excellence you beheld in it was, after all, that of a mere creature.

[14] Rom. 8:28.

This is what happened even to St. John, who had already seen so many and such wonderful visions. When the bright angel stood before him to reveal the secrets of God, he said, "And I fell down before his feet to adore him. But he saith to me, 'See thou do it not: I am thy fellow servant, and of thy brethren, who have the testimony of Jesus. Adore God.' "[15] St. Augustine[16] says that "the angel was so beautiful and glorious that St. John actually mistook him for God, and would really have given him divine worship, had not the angel prevented it by declaring who he was." From all this, we begin to see what St. John means when he tells us that we shall be like God, "because we shall see Him as He is."

∞

The vision of God will
make your soul like Him

Our likeness to God was begun on the very first day of our existence. It was gradually developed by God's grace and the sacraments and by our own cooperation with all the helps of God. But during life, the process of development was slow — so very slow, that we were at times tempted to think it had ceased altogether. But in the Beatific Vision, the process is rapid as a flash. The soul is suddenly transformed into that degree of likeness to God which it has deserved by a holy life. The soul is made to be like God, because it sees Him as He is. It is this glorious vision which contains in itself this transforming power and which assimilates the soul to God.

[15] Rev. 19:10.
[16] St. Augustine (354-430), Bishop of Hippo.

The Happiness of Heaven

In this world a deformed man may gaze upon a beautiful object without becoming beautiful thereby. A poor man may gaze upon a rich man, but remains as poor as ever. An ignorant man may gaze upon a philosopher, and nevertheless remains as ignorant as before.

It is not so in Heaven. The vision of God has a transforming power — that is, it has the power of communicating to the beholder attributes which he did not have before, or possessed only potentially. Thus the soul, because it sees God as He is, is filled to overflowing with all knowledge. It becomes beautiful with the beauty of God, rich with His wealth, holy with His holiness, and happy with His own unutterable happiness. In a word, by the vision of God, the soul is made a partaker of the divine nature, and, like a very god, it shines unto all eternity in the divine brightness.

A diamond, carefully cut and perfectly polished, glitters and shines in the sun with exceeding brilliancy. It not only reflects the light, but also absorbs it into itself, so as to shine even in the dark with the light it has absorbed. It actually becomes, as it were, a little sun, shining with its own light. It has thus become a partaker of the sun's nature, while it retains its own particular diamond nature and individuality. This is an image of what takes place in the Beatific Vision.

While it was in this world, God had polished that soul, by the sacraments and by sufferings, and now that it is in His presence and sees Him as He is, it shines and sparkles in His light with unspeakable splendor. The soul reflects and absorbs the divine light and beauty of God. It is like God, because it sees Him as He is; it is made a partaker of the divine nature, while it retains its own human nature and personal identity.

But, let us again hear Lessius. Speaking of this communication of the divine nature to man, he says, "This communication begins in this life, by the gifts of grace, especially faith, hope, and charity. By these virtues, we are not only made like to God, but God is also united to us. It is perfected, however, in the next life by the gifts of glory — namely, the light of glory, the vision of the Divinity, beatific love, and beatific joy. For, by these, we attain our highest similitude to God and become perfectly sons of God, shining like the Divinity, and exhibiting in ourselves the most excellent image of the most Holy Trinity. For by the light of glory we are made like the Father; by the vision of the Divine Essence and the Divine Persons, we become like the Son; by beatific love we are made like the Holy Spirit; by joy we become like the Godhead in beatitude, and thus the participation of the divine beatitude is completed in us."[17]

∞

Strive to perfect your soul

Now, Christian soul, meditate well on all this. Endeavor to fathom the bliss of the saints when they see themselves like God in so eminent a degree. Remember that you were created to enjoy the unspeakable happiness of seeing God and of being made a partaker of the divine nature.

But remember, too, that God, who created you without your cooperation, will not save you without it. He never will polish your soul into a jewel fit for Heaven, in spite of yourself. You must, therefore, cooperate with Him and do His holy will

---

[17] *On Divine Perfection*, Bk. 14, ch. 1.

in all things. However painful may be the trials He sends you, they are all so many strokes to take away some roughness or deformity which would prevent your soul from being perfectly like Him. Every act you perform, while in the state of grace, adds a new feature of beauty to your soul and therefore prepares it the better to receive the finishing touch in the Beatific Vision and to shine with greater splendor as a perfect image of the living God.

Chapter Three

You will be filled with knowledge

In the Beatific Vision, our intellect is glorified and our thirst for knowledge completely satisfied.

Man was created with a thirst for knowledge which can never be satiated in this world. Sin, which greatly weakened and darkened his mental faculties, has not taken away his desire and love for knowledge. And the knowledge which he acquired by eating the forbidden fruit increased rather than satisfied his thirst.

But all his efforts to reach the perfection of knowledge, even in the natural order, have been fruitless. With all his boasted discoveries in astronomy, chemistry, geology, mechanics, and other kindred sciences, his knowledge of nature's secrets is still very limited. But if he could even master every natural science and compel nature to reveal its most hidden secrets, his thirst for knowledge would still remain unsatisfied.

Let us, for the sake of illustration, imagine a man so gifted that he not only knows all that can be known about this world, but also soars beyond it and learns the exact size, distances, laws, and relations to each other of the countless worlds that shine in the blue sky. Supposing these distant orbs to be peopled like ours, imagine that this man knows the character, manners, laws, and languages of their respective inhabitants. He knows, moreover, all their sciences, and the characters of their plants, animals, and minerals. In a word, he sees and knows every star as perfectly as he knows his own house and its inmates.

What vast knowledge that man would possess! He would certainly be far more learned than all the philosophers that ever lived, taken together. But would his thirst for knowledge be completely quenched? Would he say that his mind is so completely full that he can long for no more, or that it can contain no more? No, he could never say that, for the knowledge of the creature alone can never completely fill or satisfy the mind.

We are little, and very limited, it is true, and if we are aiming at Christian perfection, we are accustomed to look upon ourselves as such. And the more often we compare our borrowed perfections with those of God, the more deeply convinced of our littleness shall we become. But yet, however little we may be, we have, in a certain sense, capacity for the infinite, and for it, only the infinite is sufficient. Hence, as all the wealth of this world could never make any man perfectly happy, so neither could the perfect knowledge of every creature perfectly satisfy his cravings after knowledge. The one is as finite as the other, and consequently, neither could do that for which the infinite alone is sufficient.

Yet, this is not all. Not only is the full knowledge of the whole natural order incapable of satisfying man's desire for knowledge, but not even all the knowledge of God and of the supernatural order, so far as they can be known in this world by faith and theology, ever did or ever could make a man say, "It is enough; I ask for no more." Indeed, the very reverse takes place. For if there is any knowledge that intensifies thirst for more, it is precisely the imperfect knowledge of God we have by faith and the contemplation of Him in His creatures.

The theologians have studied and learned much. They have thrown much light on the dark mysteries of Revelation. Yet what they know is only as a drop in the boundless ocean of God's unfathomable being. With all the vast knowledge of God which they have acquired, they are still constrained to cry out with St. Paul, "Oh, the depth of the riches of the wisdom and of the knowledge of God! How incomprehensible are His judgments, and how unsearchable His ways!"[18] Do what we may — read the Holy Scriptures, study, pray, meditate — we can never see and know God as He is, so long as we remain pilgrims in this world. The saying of St. Paul will ever remain true: "We now see through a glass in a dark manner"[19] — that is, imperfectly and unsatisfactorily.

∞

On earth, you see only the reflection of God

In the original Greek, St. Paul uses the word *mirror*, which is also the word used in the Latin Vulgate, *per speculum* — that is, by means of a mirror. The meaning, therefore, of St. Paul is not that we see through a glass by transmitted light, as when we look through a telescope, but as when we see an image reflected in a mirror.

Let us suppose a man so circumstanced in this world that he has never seen the sun, or its light, except as reflected in

[18] Rom. 11:33.
[19] 1 Cor. 13:12.

the moon. He has heard of the sun's immense size and its be-wildering distance from us, of its dazzling splendor and keen, life-imparting power, whereby it gives life, growth, and beauty to every living thing. To this man, the moon is a mirror wherein the sun is imperfectly reflected. Although he is un-able to see the sun himself, he judges from the splendor and beauty of the moon that it must be grand, glorious, and mag-nificent beyond the power of words to express.

This illustrates the meaning of St. Paul when he says that we now see God by means of a mirror. All creatures — the sun, the moon, and the stars, the vast expanse of the ocean, the earth, trees, flowers, animals, and man especially — are a grand mirror in which the perfections of God are reflected in a dark and imperfect manner. We see in them all faint reflec-tions of His divine beauty, of His wisdom, of His goodness, of His power, and of His other perfections; but as He is, we can-not see. Therefore, all the knowledge of God which we can de-rive from the contemplation of creatures, adding even all that He has been pleased to reveal of Himself, far from satisfying, rather increases the thirst of the soul for more.

∞

In Heaven, you will see God face-to-face

They who know most about God are the saints, and they are the very ones who can say, with the royal prophet, "As the hart panteth after the fountains of water, so my soul panteth after Thee, O God. My soul hath thirsted after the strong, living God; when shall I come and appear before the face of God?"[20]

---

[20] Ps. 41:2-3 (RSV = Ps. 42:1-2).

This is the continual sigh and cry of the saints, because the knowledge which they have of God in creatures, and even in their visions, does not satisfy their longings. But listen to St. Paul: "We now see through a glass in a dark manner; but then face-to-face. Now I know in part; but then I shall know even as I am known."[21]

How consoling these words of inspiration are! Yes, in Heaven, we shall see God as He is, face-to-face. We shall see Him in all His adorable perfections by a clear and unclouded perception of His Divine Essence. We shall gaze with unspeakable delight and rapture upon that "beauty, ever ancient and ever new."[22] We shall drink in all knowledge at its living source — unmingled with error or doubt. All the darkness and ignorance caused by sin will forever vanish in the light of God's countenance, as the darkness of night disappears before the rising sun.

We shall then see, as it is, the august and awe-inspiring mystery of the most Holy Trinity — the deepest, the sublimest, and the most incomprehensible of all those that God ever revealed to man. We shall then see the eternal Father, ever begetting His only Son, and the Holy Spirit ever proceeding from both Father and Son. We shall then see how They are really three distinct Persons, and yet one undivided Essence. We shall see, face-to-face, and as He is, this great, eternal God, in the eternity of His duration, in the abysses of His unsearchable judgments, in the sweetness of His goodness, in the tenderness of His mercies, in the spotlessness of His sanctity, in the

---

[21] 1 Cor. 13:12.
[22] St. Augustine, *Confessions*, Bk. 10, ch. 27.

severity of His justice, in the might of His irresistible power, in the charms of His captivating beauty, and in the splendor of His majesty and glory. In a word, we shall no longer see God as He is reflected in the mirror of creation, but as He is in Himself.

This is the vision which no mortal has seen, or can see in this world. This is the vision which pours torrents of knowledge into our souls and fills them to overflowing. No more searching of books; no more wasting away of health and strength in the pursuit of knowledge; no more going to learned men, as the beggar goes to the rich for bread. No more perplexing and torturing doubts that perhaps we do not have the truth. The light of glory will have opened our eyes, and we will see all truth as it is and will become like God in knowledge, because we will see Him as He is.

∞

You will see yourself as you are

But this is not yet all. The glorification of our intellect will not only enable us to see God as He is; it will also unveil us to ourselves, and make us see ourselves as we are.

In our present state of existence, we are a mystery to ourselves. In spite of the numberless learned works written on the mind and the laws by which it operates, our knowledge of the mind is still very limited. We see the human soul only as reflected in a mirror — that is, in its outward manifestations.

Thus, when we read a magnificent poem; or when we gaze upon a noble ship ploughing the waters of the deep, or riding safely through a fearful storm; or when we look upon grand churches, palaces, and works of art — all these are as mirrors, which reflect the greatness, wisdom, power, and ingenuity of the human soul. Again, when we enter orphan asylums, or other institutions for the unfortunate and destitute of every description, we may view them as mirrors which reflect the moral goodness of the soul. But the soul itself as it is, we cannot see. It is as invisible to us as God Himself.

In Heaven, we shall know and see ourselves as we are. For, as St. Paul tells us, "Then I shall know even as I am known." We shall then see and know that beautiful, living image of the Eternal in our soul's very essence. We shall see it clothed with a surpassing beauty, adorned with the gems of grace and good works, and shining in the presence of God like a star. This sight of ourselves and of our exceeding beauty will kindle in us none other than sentiments of unbounded gratitude to God, who is the giver of our existence and of all that we possess. Here again, as well as in the knowledge of God, the human intellect will rest satisfied, because its thirst for the complete knowledge of self will be quenched in the Beatific Vision.

∞

You will see other creatures as they truly are

Besides seeing ourselves as we are, we shall see the beautiful angels, our elder brothers in creation. We shall also see, as they are, our fellowmen, who are now as much a mystery to us as we are to ourselves. We shall likewise see all other creatures as they are in their very essence, and not as they now appear to us. We shall see all things in the "one God and Father of all, who is above all, and through all, and in us all."[23] Thus shall

---

[23] Eph. 4:6.

our souls be filled to overflowing with all knowledge from its living source, which is God Himself, the eternal Truth.

Before closing this chapter I must remark, for fear of being misunderstood, that when we say the blessed will see all things in God, we do not mean that they will really possess all knowledge. We are finite beings and, consequently, essentially unable to possess any attribute or perfection in an infinite degree. We can no more possess all knowledge than we can be clothed with all power, all holiness, all beauty, or any other perfection in an infinite degree. All these attributes belong to God alone. Even the angels, who are so superior to us, do not know everything.[24]

When we say, therefore, that we shall see all things in God, we simply mean that each one's capacity, great or small, shall be completely filled, and that he shall desire nothing more. When we fill many vessels with water, the smallest is as full as the largest. So it is in Heaven. Each one shall know according to his individual capacity, which the light of glory will give him. Each one shall be filled to overflowing and desire no more. But we will say more on this when we come to speak of the degrees of glory.

[24] Cf. *Summa Theologica*, Suppl., Q. 92, art. 3.

Chapter Four

You will enjoy perfect love

In the Beatific Vision, our will is also to be glorified, and then we shall be happy in loving and being loved.

We have seen in the foregoing chapter that our intellectual faculties are glorified and that our natural thirst for knowledge is forever quenched. But we have another faculty, called the will, or the loving power of the soul. This faculty is also to be glorified in the Beatific Vision. Then our continual desire for happiness, which we vainly sought in creatures, will be completely gratified.

We shall now see that, in the Beatific Vision, our will or moral nature is elevated, ennobled, and made like God by a participation of His sanctity, beatitude, and love. But let us first cast a glance at ourselves, as we are now in our fallen state.

Original Sin has turned man's will from God's

When our first parents revolted against God, they abandoned the eternal rule of rectitude, which is God's will. Their passions, which heretofore had been under the control of reason, revolted against them, and their will was turned away from God. We, their children, have inherited all the consequences of their Fall. We seek ourselves inordinately and follow our own capricious will, which leads us into excesses, at which we blush in our sober moments. We stubbornly persist in seeking our happiness in creatures, although reason itself loudly proclaims that in them happiness cannot be found. Evidently, then, our will has been sadly perverted in the Fall of our first parents.

One of the objects of the Christian religion was to bring our will back to a conformity with the divine will and to cause it to love God above all things. Yet, in spite of its manifold teachings, in spite, too, of the sacraments and the many graces we daily receive, in spite of prayer, meditation, and other spiritual exercises, this grand object is only partially attained in this world.

For we find our perverse will again and again rising in rebellion against God. When a command is imposed upon us which does not chime in with our wishes, private interests, views, or natural inclinations, we not unfrequently must drag ourselves by sheer force to perform what is commanded. And if we do obey, it is often only after doing all in our power, by excuse or pretext, to escape the obligation of obeying. Indeed, we all can say with the apostle, "I am delighted with the law of God, according to the inward man; but I see another law in my members, fighting against the law of my mind, and captivating me under the law of sin that is in my members."[25]

What a tyranny this law of sin exercises over the will — even of holy persons! How often do they discover, on close

[25] Rom. 7:22-23.

examination, that their will has departed from the eternal rule, which is the will of God! How often do they find that they had been seeking their own glory instead of God's! After doing really great things, which they fancied were done purely for God, they find, to their grief, that, to a great extent, they had been secretly and artfully seeking themselves and their own glory. And they have reason to fear that they have already received their reward in that human applause which they sought, or in which they took such complacency when it came unsought.

It is said that persons who have been bitten by a viper, and who have nevertheless recovered by the application of timely remedies, are never again the same in health as they were before. At times they are swollen, or feel acute pains, or have a morbid and depraved appetite for what they should not eat. At other times, they feel a general languor, which takes away all their energy, so that whatever they do requires a most painful effort. Evidently, some of the poison is still lurking in their system, and so long as it remains there, these infirmities will never be entirely healed.

So it is with us, from a moral point of view. Our human nature was bitten and poisoned by the infernal serpent in the earthly paradise, and although a powerful antidote was given us in the Redemption, some of the venom remained in us. And as long as we live here below, we shall feel its effects. We shall always feel the sting of concupiscence and retain an inclination to evil — to seek ourselves inordinately and to follow our own will. We shall always experience a certain languor in the practice of virtue, which involves a continual effort and struggle.

The Happiness of Heaven

∞

Your will be in conformity with God's

What an exquisite consolation it is to us to be assured that none of this poison will follow us into Heaven! Yes, the day will come — blessed and glorious day! — when all that perversity of will, all that inclination to evil, and all the passions of our depraved nature will be no more! All these will die in our temporal death and be buried — never to rise again in our glorified bodies. The Beatific Vision will glorify our will and change us, as it were, into new creatures.

Then shall we find ourselves joyfully willing to do what God wills, as He wills it, and because He so wills it — without the least repugnance on our part. We shall no longer have peculiar views, private interests, or natural inclinations that clash with the will and interests of God. His divine will and our will shall become so totally one that we shall seem to have no will of our own — so completely and, at the same time, so sweetly, shall it be identified with the will and good pleasure of God. In a word, as our intellect is elevated by the light of glory and filled with the purest knowledge in the Beatific Vision, so also our will is purified, sanctified, and made like God's will, in rectitude and perfect sanctity.

∞

You will love and be loved perfectly

Not only shall our will become holy and conformed to God's will, but we shall also love God above all things, purely, unselfishly, ardently, and for His own blessed sake. And in that love we shall at last find the perfect happiness we vainly sought in the love of creatures.

Human love is a source of partial happiness in this world, and it is in this human love, as in a mirror, that we see faint reflections of the unspeakable happiness which will inebriate our souls in the Beatific Vision. But they are emphatically faint reflections, for whether it be conjugal, parental, or fraternal love, or whether it be the love of pure friendship — whether it be even elevated by grace to the supernatural virtue of charity — human love never did, and never will, bestow perfect happiness in this world. It depends for its existence and perfection on conditions which can never be completely fulfilled in our present state of imperfection; and, therefore, the short-lived happiness to which human love gives birth is always mingled with a certain amount of bitterness.

It is in Heaven, and only in Heaven, that all the conditions of love can be fulfilled, and, hence, it is there only that love will produce pure and perfect happiness, unmingled with the disappointments, cruel misunderstandings, and insufficiency of human love.

∞

In Heaven, love is mutual

First of all, the love of Heaven is essentially mutual. The vision of God not only reveals to the soul His divine beauty, goodness, wisdom, and numberless other perfections, which captivate the soul, and set it on fire with a seraphic love, but it also reveals the intense and mysterious love of God for the soul. The sight of that divine love produces in the soul the happiness which the heart of man cannot conceive.

If a great king should speak kindly to a poor peasant, smile upon him, and even show him a real affection, a happiness which he never experienced before would take possession of that peasant's heart. A thrill of joy would run through every fiber of his frame. He would be a new man and live a new life, simply because a great one of this world had smiled upon him and condescended to love him.

This is a faint reflection of that undying thrill of joy, of that unspeakable happiness which the loving smile of God will produce upon the soul. For, in the Beatific Vision, the soul sees clearly that, in spite of its littleness and insignificance, which it never saw as it now does, in spite, too, of the sins and imperfections which had stained its beauty while in the flesh, the great and thrice-holy God loves the soul infinitely more tenderly and sincerely than either father or mother, or any other creature ever did. Not only does the soul see the intense love of God beaming upon it now, but it sees, moreover, that He loved it from eternity, when it existed as yet only in the divine mind. Yes, the soul sees itself lying in the bosom of the Eternal, with His mysterious love brooding over it, and giving it existence in the fullness of time.

This is truly and emphatically for the soul a Beatific Vision. It is vain for us to endeavor to fathom the exquisite happiness which this vision of God's love produces in the soul. For, if the mere smile of a king has the power of infusing joy into the heart of a poor and insignificant person, what shall we say of the smile of God, who is the King of kings? What shall we say of His affectionate, paternal embrace? What shall we say of the joy and happiness that flow into the soul when He presses the soul to His bosom, gives it the kiss of peace, and calls it His own beloved child? What shall we say of the soul's exceeding happiness, when He makes the soul a partaker of His divine nature and unites it to Himself more intimately than two creatures ever could be united in this world?

These are all secrets of Heaven. They are simply unspeakable, because they are beyond our present powers of comprehension. Eye hath not seen them, ear hath not heard them, nor hath it entered into the heart of man to conceive them.[26] We shall, therefore, make no further attempt to express what no human tongue can utter. But we may say that, as a pure and mutual love produces the greatest happiness we know of in this world, so also the mutual love which exists between the soul and God in the Beatific Vision is the source of the most perfect happiness possible.

∞

In Heaven love is unfailing

But there is another feature of that unspeakable happiness that we must now consider. Love must not only be mutual to produce happiness; there must also be neither fear nor suspicion that either of the parties will prove false. Everyone knows that when a suspicion of that nature fastens upon the mind of one who loves, his happiness is at an end, and there is no telling to what extravagant excesses his jealousy may lead him.

This imperfection, which blasts so much happiness in this world, will never find its way into our heavenly home. For the soul sees that He who loved it from eternity will continue to do so everlastingly. And it sees not only the utter impossibility that God will ever despise it, but also the impossibility that it will ever prove false to Him.

[26] Cf. 1 Cor. 2:9.

It not only sees God as He is, but also sees everything else as it is. However beautiful, therefore, creatures may be in Heaven, the soul always sees in God a beauty and perfection so vastly, so infinitely superior, that it is impossible for it to be captivated by creatures, as it was in this world. The soul loves all the companions of its bliss, it is true, but it loves them all in God and for God. It loves them because they are His and because He loves them. It loves them, too, because they are so holy, so beautiful, and so much like God, and, therefore, deserving of its love.

But the soul's chief, absorbing love is centered in God and remains centered there forever. Never can there come a day when the soul will see a growing coldness in God toward it; never shall there dawn a day when the soul will discover in itself a growing coldness toward God; and, consequently, there never shall be a day when the soul's exceeding happiness will fade away or be lessened. Rather, the soul sees the dawn of a glorious day when its happiness will be increased, perfected, and completed in the resurrection of the body — a day when other joys and pleasures will be added to those it now enjoys in the Beatific Vision.

Chapter Five

You will be beautified and glorified

We have seen in the foregoing chapters that, in the Beatific Vision, the human soul sees, loves, and enjoys God, and that its essential happiness consists in that unfailing, blessed vision. But, although the blessedness it now enjoys is far greater than words can express, that blessedness is not yet integral or complete, and will not be until when the soul is again clothed in its own body, beautified, and glorified after the likeness of its Savior's body.

However, although the soul's happiness is not yet complete, you must not therefore imagine that the least shadow of sadness or unhappiness hangs over it. For, as we have seen, its will is now totally conformed to God's will. It follows that, although the soul sees other joys and pleasures in store for it, and desires them, these desires do not in the least mar its exceeding happiness. The soul wills the resurrection of its body as God wills it, and because He wills it, and also because its body is absolutely necessary to complete its human nature, which essentially consists of both soul and body.

We shall begin our meditations on the resurrection of the body by first contemplating the beauty and splendor of the glorified body.

The Happiness of Heaven

∞

Matter can be perfected and refined

In order to form some idea of the perfect beauty and splendor of form which is in store for us, we must first look at some of the transformations which take place in the natural order. These will aid us, very materially, in arriving at a conception, more or less perfect, of the glorious transformation which the power of God will work in us at the resurrection.

When we examine the kingdoms of nature, we discover that the gross matter which surrounds us in shapeless masses is capable of forms and organizations so perfect, refined, and beautiful, that we may, in some sense, call these forms glorified matter. It is, certainly, matter glorified far above inferior forms in the natural order. Let us take a few examples.

What is the diamond? It is nothing more than crystallized carbon, or charcoal. There is nothing in the whole range of science which can be so easily and so positively proved as this. The famous diamond Koh-i-noor, meaning "mountain of light," which now sparkles in the British crown, and which is worth millions of dollars, could, in a few moments, be reduced to a thimbleful of worthless coal dust. Yet, how great a difference, in appearance and value, between that precious gem and a thimbleful of coal dust!

Again, what are other gems, such as the ruby, the sapphire, the topaz, the emerald, and others? They are nothing more than crystallized clay or sand, with a trifling quantity of metallic oxide or rust, which gives to each one its particular color. Yet, what a difference between these sparkling and costly jewels and the shapeless clod of sand which we trample underfoot!

If we now look for a moment into the vegetable kingdom, we see this glorification of matter still more wonderfully displayed. Of what are all plants composed? They are all composed of four elements of matter, which have no remarkable beauty of their own. In scientific language they are called carbon or charcoal, oxygen, hydrogen, and nitrogen. By the power and the laws of life, these are transformed into that endless variety of beauty and color, odor and taste, so striking in the vegetable world. Hence, the most beautiful flowers and their exquisite perfumes, as well as the delicious fruits to which they give birth, are all made of the very same elements of matter as the bark, the wood, and the root of the tree that bears them. Yet, what a difference between the coarse tree and the delicate flower! What a difference, too, between the tasteless bark or the wood of the tree and the luscious fruit that hangs in clusters from its branches!

Now if, in the natural order, God can and does transform coarse and shapeless matter into forms so beautiful and so glorious, what shall we say of the beauty and perfection into which He will change our vile bodies! For all these transformations which we now witness belong to the natural order and are the result of the laws which govern matter in this world of imperfection, whereas our transformation in the resurrection depends on the immediate act of God's almighty power.

The difference, therefore, between our present corruptible body and the glorified body, will be greater by far than the difference we now see between charcoal and the diamond, or between the exquisitely shaped flower and the coarse shrub that bears it.

∞

Your body will be glorified

Having said this much to aid us in forming some idea of the glorified body, we shall now proceed to examine one of its attributes, which St. Paul mentions when he says, "It is sown in dishonor; it shall rise in glory."[27] Our bodies are indeed sown in dishonor, in the company of worms, and a prey to corruption in life. They are honored by the presence of an immortal spirit, the very image of the living God. They are honored by the Holy Spirit, who makes them His temple. They are honored, too, by the presence of Jesus Christ, who makes them His tabernacle every time we receive Him in Holy Communion. But death strikes them down; the spirit flees; our bodies lie cold and motionless, and corruption begins to assert its empire over them. Our nearest and dearest friends hasten to throw them into the dark and silent grave, where they return to their original dust. Then, indeed, our bodies are "sown in dishonor." But in the fullness of time, these same dishonored bodies "shall rise in glory."

This word *glory* is one of great and manifold meanings in Holy Scripture. In this particular place and connection, it means excellence and beauty, accompanied with a shining splendor. Thus, that our bodies "shall rise in glory" means, first, that they shall rise perfect in beauty and symmetry of form and totally free from the defects and blemishes entailed by sin. This perfect beauty of form is evidently involved in the promise of rising conformable to the glorious body of our blessed Savior, "who will reform the body of our lowness, made

---

[27] 1 Cor. 15:43 (King James Version).

like the body of His glory, according to the operation whereby He is also able to subdue all things unto Himself."[28]

The human body was created perfect in the beginning. It was the masterpiece of God's power and wisdom in this world. But sin dishonored and disfigured it. It gave birth to a host of infirmities, which mar its original beauty and in some cases change it even into a monster. Still, in spite of sin, it yet retains, in many individuals, much of its primitive comeliness. But however perfect in form and feature anyone may be, there is always some deficiency; some member, organ, or feature is slightly distorted, imperfect, or out of proportion with the rest.

On the resurrection day, all these defects and blemishes will disappear, and the human body will again, far more than in the beginning, be a masterpiece of God's creative power, wisdom, and love. For every member, organ, and feature will then be exquisitely shaped and proportioned, so as to harmonize into a perfect whole of surpassing beauty, without defect or deficiency of any kind.

Oh! with what rapturous delight will the soul reunite itself with that beautiful body and make it its temple forever! The body was the companion of its sorrows and its joys in this world. But it was, too, a body of sin and death, and the soul had, perhaps more than once, sighed and prayed to be delivered from it.[29] But now that the body is purified, beautified, and glorified, the soul re-enters it with joy, because it has become the fit companion of a beatified spirit. The fond mother meeting her long-lost child, and, in the joy of her heart,

---

[28] Phil. 3:21.
[29] Cf. Rom. 7:24.

pressing him to her bosom, is a faint image of the joy which the soul will experience in the reunion with its glorified body.

But this is not all. St. Thomas maintains that, besides rising in perfect beauty of form, all the just must rise in the bloom and vigor of youth; otherwise our bodies would not, according to promise, rise "conformable to the glorious body" of Jesus Christ.[30] From this doctrine it follows that all defect, or appearance of old age, as well as the infirmities and deficiencies of infancy, will be completely removed, and all the saints will enjoy the full perfection of human nature.

What consolation there is in all these glorious promises! To be forever young and vigorous, forever blessed with perfect health of mind and body, to be forever beyond the reach of time, which destroys all beauty here below, to be clothed with a body that shall forever be a stranger to suffering: these are some of the joys in store for the children of God in the resurrection of the body.

However, this is not all. Rising in glory means something more than rising in mere beauty of form, bloom of youth, and the complete perfection of human nature. It also implies a radiant brilliancy with which the just will shine on the resurrection day. This is one of the meanings of glory in the language of Scripture. Take the following as one instance out of many: "And when Aaron spoke to all the assembly of the children of Israel, they looked toward the wilderness; and, behold, the glory of the Lord appeared in a cloud."[31] That is, a brilliant and dazzling splendor burst forth in the heavens. So it was also

---

[30] *Summa Theologica*, Suppl., Q. 81, art. 1.
[31] Exod. 16:10.

when Jesus was glorified in His transfiguration: "His face did shine as the sun, and His garments became white as snow."[32] Moreover, as a general rule, when celestial inhabitants appeared in this world, they were surrounded with a halo of brilliant light, as we read of the angels who appeared at the birth of Christ[33] and of those who appeared to the holy women who were going to embalm the body of Jesus.[34] Hence it is that in the paintings of Christian art, the head or the whole body of Christ, of the Blessed Virgin, and of the saints is always surrounded by this halo of light.

This is the light, the brilliancy, which is promised to the saints by our blessed Lord Himself when He says, "Then shall the just shine as the sun in the kingdom of their Father."[35] Thus shall the soul that is united to God in the Beatific Vision, and already a partaker of the divine nature, communicate its own dazzling splendor to the body and surround it with an aureola of glory, which will form a portion of the soul's blessedness forevermore.

∞

Your heavenly beauty will reflect your holiness

But, although all the just must rise in glory and in the perfection of human nature, you must not, therefore, infer that all shall rise in the same degree of beauty and splendor of form. For, as the resurrection is a reward to the just, it follows that

[32] Mark 9:2 (RSV = Mark 9:3).
[33] Luke 2:9
[34] Matt. 28:1-3.
[35] Matt. 13:43.

each one shall have a body glorified in proportion to his own individual merits. Any contrary doctrine would sound like heresy. If you were told, for instance, that the murderer who dies on the scaffold, after making an act of perfect contrition, will rise on the last day with a body as beautiful and glorious as that of the Blessed Virgin, or of the Apostles, martyrs, and holy virgins, your whole soul would revolt at such a doctrine. You would maintain that if the resurrection is a reward to the just, the beauty of their bodies should bear some proportion to their merits.

You would certainly be right in maintaining this, for it is the very doctrine taught by St. Paul when he says, "One is the glory of the sun, another the glory of the moon, and another the glory of the stars, for star differeth from star in glory: so also in the resurrection of the dead."[36] Each one, therefore, shall rise in that particular degree of glory which he has deserved by the more or less holy life he has led in this world.

It will no longer be as it is in this world, where personal beauty is a free gift of God, but no reward. Hence, we see personal beauty in pagans and infidels, as well as in Christians. Its possession does not, in the least, denote sanctity, nor does its absence denote moral depravity. Therefore, beautiful persons may be very wicked, while deformed ones may be very holy.

It will not be so after the resurrection. Perfect personal beauty, accompanied by a heavenly splendor, being one of the rewards in store for the children of God, will then denote sanctity in the just. The more holy they have been in this life,

[36] 1 Cor. 15:41-42.

the more beautiful and conformable to the glorious body of Jesus they shall be in the life to come.

Now, Christian reader, do you wish to possess faultless personal beauty in your heavenly home? Do you desire not only to increase your own blessedness, but also to be even an ornament in the kingdom of your Father? No doubt you do. Well, you have the means in your hands. Lead a holy life, a life of purity and perfect charity. Endeavor to reproduce in yourself the virtues which Jesus taught and practiced, and when the angel's trumpet calls the dead to life,[37] your body, which must first be sown in dishonor, shall rise in that degree of beauty which you have deserved by the holiness of your life.

[37] Cf. 1 Cor. 15:52.

Chapter Six

∽

You will no longer
experience earthly limitations

Having seen the personal beauty and splendor with which the just will rise on the last day, we shall now examine some other attributes of the glorified body. St. Paul tells us: "It is sown a natural body; it shall rise a spiritual body."[38]

Rising a spiritual body does not mean that the bodies of the just shall be changed into spirits. Our bodies, which are material by nature, must remain so forever. They must rise in conformity to the glorious body of Jesus Christ, "who will reform the body of our lowness made like to the body of His glory."[39]

And what kind of a body did Jesus Christ have when He rose triumphant over death and Hell? It was certainly His own material body of real flesh and blood, and not a spirit. When He appeared to His Apostles, as St. Luke tells us, "they, being troubled and affrighted, supposed that they saw a spirit. And He said to them, 'Why are you troubled, and why do these thoughts arise in your hearts? See my hands and feet, that it is I myself; handle and see, for a spirit hath not flesh and bones as

[38] 1 Cor. 15:44.
[39] Phil. 3:21.

you see me have.' "[40] Assuredly, here is a true body of flesh and blood and bone, and not a spiritual one in the sense that matter does or can become a spirit. It is the very same body in which He suffered such terrible tortures and agonies during His bitter Passion.

So shall we rise on the last day, in our own material body of flesh and blood, with every organ and member glorified and made conformable to the body of Jesus Christ. According to the teachings of St. Thomas, our bodies shall rise of the same nature as they now are. For glory does not change or destroy nature, but perfects it.[41] Evidently, then, rising a spiritual body does not mean that our bodies are to be changed into spirits.

What, then, does it mean? It means that, while retaining their essential material nature, they will be clothed with properties which naturally belong only to spirits and not to bodies. These we shall now examine.

∞

Your risen body will need no food, drink, or sleep
In the first place, rising a spiritual body implies that the glorified body will no longer need food, drink, and sleep to sustain life and strength, as it now does. The risen body will, therefore, in this respect, become like a spirit, which needs neither food nor drink. Eating is a necessity of the present life and makes our bodies animal. This necessity will no longer exist after the resurrection.

[40] Luke 24:37-39.
[41] Cf. *Summa Theologica*, I, Q. 62, art. 7; *Summa Contra Gentiles*, Bk. 4, ch. 84.

You will no longer experience limitations

When we reflect upon this, it seems to us that nearly one-half of human life and its energies is expended upon providing, preparing, and eating food. Fields must be sown and crops must be raised. Grain must be ground. Cattle must be cared for almost as children. Ships must cross and recross the ocean. And all this to prepare food for our vile bodies. What a slavery this is! Instead of giving its time to the development of its faculties and the contemplation of God and His works, the soul, that noble image of the living God, must provide and prepare food for the body. Rising a spiritual body will forever emancipate us from this slavery.

But although it is true that there shall be no more eating and drinking in Heaven, as we now understand these two actions, you must not infer from this that the sense of taste shall not be gratified in the blessed. It most certainly will be, as well as every other sense of the human body, although not by the corruptible food of the present life.

When the butterfly was a caterpillar, it devoured green leaves with pleasure and avidity. They were its very life. But now that it is changed into a beautiful butterfly, it lives on the honey and exquisite perfume of flowers. If you offer it those same leaves that it loved so much while a caterpillar, it scorns them and refuses even to touch them, for they are now unable to give the butterfly any pleasure in its transformed state.

So shall it be with us after the resurrection. Our tastes shall be so refined that we shall scorn the low animal pleasures which are fit only for our present corruptible bodies. What a difference there is between the coarse green leaf, which is the food of the caterpillar, and the exquisite honey of the blushing rose, which is the food of the butterfly! There is a still greater difference between the creatures that now gratify our senses and those that are reserved in Heaven to gratify our glorified senses after the resurrection.

But there is yet another slavery besides that of eating and drinking from which we shall be delivered by rising a spiritual body. It is the slavery of sleep, which takes up nearly one-third of our lives. We all know by experience that it takes only a few hours of heavy physical labor or assiduous mental application to exhaust all our mental energies and bodily strength. And, whether we like it or not, we must sleep six or seven hours in order to regain our lost strength and to be ourselves again. How many saints have grieved over this necessity of our nature! Often have they desired to spend the nights in the contemplation of God, but in spite of their endeavors, they were overpowered by sleep. The spirit, indeed, was willing, but the flesh was weak.[42]

This imperative necessity of our animal bodies will be totally removed by their rising as spiritual bodies. Spirits have no need of sleep; their energies are never exhausted by the manifold acts they constantly perform. They live in the continual enjoyment of that supernatural strength with which they were clothed the moment the vision of God flashed upon them.

It is this wonderful strength which will be poured out, as it were, over our bodies at the resurrection. For, as St. Paul says of our body, "It is sown in weakness; it shall rise in power."[43] Hence, however intense may be the application of our mental faculties or of our physical powers in Heaven, we shall ever

[42] Cf. Matt. 26:41.
[43] 1 Cor. 15:43.

remain strangers to the well-known feelings of fatigue and prostration. All our energies shall ever remain fresh and unimpaired, and their continual exercise shall be the never-failing source of the most exquisite enjoyment.

∞

Your body and spirit will be in harmony

In the second place, rising a spiritual body implies vastly more than the mere emancipation from the necessities of nature. It means, besides, that the body will be totally subject to the spirit and, consequently, that concupiscence and other inordinate passions, which now war against the spirit, shall no longer exist. This is one of the most consoling promises to persons who are endeavoring to lead a holy life. Their present corruptible body, in which "the law of sin"[44] resides, is an enemy that is ever warring against the spirit. Often have they cried out with St. Paul: "Unhappy man that I am, who will deliver me from the body of this death? The grace of God, by Jesus Christ our Lord."[45]

Yes, the fullness of grace will have come at last, and the body of sin and death will be no more. It will have changed into a spiritual body, which will be not only totally subject to the spirit, but will even aid and perfect it, in all its intellectual operations, as well as in its moral affections. The spiritual body will therefore be no longer a burden and a temptation; it will have become like a spirit, which cannot be enslaved to inordinate animal passions or instincts.

[44] Rom. 7:23.
[45] Rom. 7:24-25.

The Happiness of Heaven

What a blessedness is here promised to us! No more involuntary cravings after forbidden pleasures; no more of those involuntary thoughts and inclinations which are so humiliating to pure souls; no more danger of being turned away from God by the beauty of creatures; no more wandering of the mind from His presence. In a word, the spiritual body will be totally subject to the spirit, and "the law of sin," which received its birth at the Fall of our first parents, will be totally destroyed.

∞

Your body will have the powers of agility and subtility

Rising a spiritual body means, in the third place, that the matter of which the body is now composed will become so refined and delicately organized as, in some sense, to approach the nature of a spirit, while retaining its essential material nature. Our body will therefore lose its material grossness, roughness of texture, and weight and will be clothed with the attributes of agility and subtility.

Agility implies the power of transporting ourselves from place to place with the rapidity of thought. In this world we can, in the twinkling of an eye, send our thoughts on the wings of electricity across a whole continent or the vast expanse of the ocean. After the resurrection, we shall possess that power in our very bodies, because they shall rise spiritual bodies, entirely under the control of the soul.

Subtility means that our risen bodies will be endowed with the power of penetrating all things, even the hardest substances, as easily as the sun's rays penetrate a clear crystal. This is the power which our blessed Lord possessed and exercised when He rose from the dead without removing the stone that covered the mouth of the sepulcher.[46] He simply passed through it with His glorified body. Again, after eight days, when the Apostles were gathered together, "Jesus cometh, the doors being shut, and stood in the midst, and said, 'Peace be to you.' "[47] This subtility is a supernatural gift with which we shall be clothed, because we must rise conformable to the glorious body of Jesus Christ.

These, then, are some of the attributes of a spiritual body. They are evidently the natural properties of spirits. But God will clothe the bodies of His children with them, as a reward for their love of Him and the holy lives they have led in this world.

---

[46] Cf. Matt. 28:2-6.
[47] John 20:26.

Chapter Seven

∽

You will be free from suffering and death

Besides the attributes which immediately flow from the fact that our natural bodies will rise spiritualized, there are two more qualities, which we shall now consider — namely, the impassibility and immortality of our risen bodies.

Impassibility implies the total loss of the power of suffering. What an enormous capacity we have for suffering! The power of receiving pleasure through our senses is only as a drop in the ocean when compared with our manifold capacity for suffering in every faculty of the soul, in every organ, member, and nerve of our frame. Every one of them is susceptible to tortures, which, while endured, make the enjoyment of life and its pleasures impossible. A violent headache or a burning fever drives a man almost to distraction and destroys any pleasure he might otherwise experience. What consolation, therefore, to think that this body of suffering shall rise impassible! No more disease, no more pain or pang, no more suffering, either of mind or body, for we shall enter a new world from which suffering is forever banished.

St. John had a glimpse of this new world, when he said, "And I saw a new Heaven and a new earth. For the first Heaven and the first earth were gone. . . . And I heard a great voice from the throne, saying: Behold the tabernacle of God with men, and He shall dwell with them. . . . And God shall wipe away all the tears from their eyes; and death shall be no more, nor mourning, nor crying, nor sorrow shall be anymore, for the former things are passed away."[48]

It was the thought of rising in glory, with a body free from suffering, that gave comfort to the holy man Job when the storm of adversity had burst upon him. Listen to his beautiful words: "I know that my Redeemer liveth, and in the last day, I shall rise out of the earth. And I shall be clothed again with my skin, and in my flesh I shall see my God, whom I myself shall see, and not another. This my hope is laid up in my bosom."[49] Lay up that hope in your bosom as he did, and when the storm of adversity bursts upon you, the thought of rising in a glorified, impassible body, and in a new world, will give you patience and resignation.

But rising with the gift of impassibility does not mean that our bodies will be unfeeling as marble statues. It means only that they shall be free from the power of suffering; but that does not exclude the power of receiving pleasure. Glory does not destroy nature, but perfects it. The bodies of the blessed will remain sensible to impressions from suitable objects, and, according to St. Thomas, the blessed will use their senses for enjoyment in all that is not repugnant to a state of incorruption.[50]

---

[48] Rev. 21:1, 3-4.
[49] Job 19:25-27.
[50] *Summa Contra Gentiles*, Bk. 4, ch. 86.

∞

Your risen body will be incorruptible

We now come to consider the crowning glory of all the glorious supernatural attributes with which God will clothe our
bodies on the last day. I say it is the crowning glory, for the
splendor of form, the vigor of youth, and the complete perfection of our human nature — which are all included in the
promise of rising conformable to the glorified body of Jesus
Christ — would scarcely be worth working for or possessing,
unless they were accompanied with the promise of incorrupt-
ibility. Indeed, of what use would be the rising with the bloom
of youth and health on our cheek, and in perfect beauty of
form, if time could again destroy them — as in this world!

But there is no danger that the destroyer will ever enter our
heavenly home. Listen to St. Paul. Speaking again of the body,
he says, "It is sown in corruption; it shall rise in incorruption."[51]

Our bodies, as now constituted, are corruptible by their
very nature. The elements of matter which compose them are
held together by the laws of life and not by their natural affini-
ties. Hence, from the very first moment of our existence to our
death, there is a continual struggle between the laws of life
and those that govern inorganic matter. For a time, vigorous
young life claims the supremacy, and the body grows to its degree of beauty and strength attainable in this world. But soon
the laws of decay and corruption begin to assert their empire.
Beauty of feature and form gradually fade away; elasticity of
limb gives way to the decrepitude of old age; and finally the
whole frame becomes a burden under which nature groans and

[51] 1 Cor. 15:42.

totters, until it falls into the gloomy grave, where corruption destroys every remaining vestige of beauty, and even of the human form.

On the resurrection day, we not only shall rise in splendor and perfection of form, but we shall also be transferred to another world, whose laws are in perfect harmony with the laws of life and into which corruption shall never enter.

In the present world, we already see things which, as far as nature's laws go, are incorruptible. The diamond, for instance, is the most incorruptible of all known substances; and unless the existing laws of nature should change, when the angel sounds the trumpet to announce to the world that time shall be no more, the splendid Koh-i-noor and other diamonds will glitter as brilliantly as they now do. These beautiful gems are therefore a faint image of our glorified bodies, which shall not only rise in perfection of form, but shall also be totally incorruptible. They shall forever be beyond the reach of death, decay, and corruption, resplendent in themselves and increasing the very beauty of Heaven, as sparkling gems enhance the beauty of a royal crown.

Yes, this vile and corruptible body must be changed into an incorruptible one. It must rise like the body of Jesus Christ, who, "rising again from the dead, dieth no more; death shall no more have dominion over Him."[52] According to the beautiful and forcible words of the apostle: "This corruptible must put on incorruption; and this mortal must put on immortality. And when this mortal hath put on immortality, then shall come to pass the saying that is written: Death is swallowed up

[52] Rom. 6:9.

in victory. O death, where is thy victory? O death, where is thy sting?"[53]

∞

Your body and soul will together enjoy happiness

These, then, are some of the supernatural gifts with which God will clothe the bodies of the just on the last day. They are so great in themselves, that it would almost seem they should be worth working for even if there were no Beatific Vision. Yet, if taken separately, they are, so to speak, the mere external ornaments and finish of the happiness which the heart of man cannot conceive.

These glorious attributes of the risen body perfect and complete the happiness of man. As the soul and body reunited in glory form one human creature, so the happiness of the soul and body is one. After the resurrection, the beatitude of Heaven can no longer be separated into the happiness of the soul in the Beatific Vision, and then the pleasures of the body through the glorified senses, as if there were two distinct beatitudes, or as if the soul and body were two distinct individuals. Whatever happiness comes from the union of the soul with God in the Beatific Vision, and whatever pleasures may reach the soul through the glorified senses, or from our communion with the saints, or the contemplation of the sacred humanity of Jesus Christ, the Blessed Virgin Mary, and other saints, it is all one happiness enjoyed by our human nature, which is one.

[53] 1 Cor. 15:53-55.

Chapter Eight

You will enjoy complete happiness

Now that the soul is again clothed in its body, glorified after the likeness of Christ's body, other pleasures and joys, besides those we have already contemplated in the Beatific Vision, claim our attention. They are the pleasures of the glorified senses, which, along with the Beatific Vision, are to gratify every rational appetite and craving of our human nature. And thus the whole man, in soul and body, will enjoy the complete happiness of Heaven. But, in order to form a correct idea of these additional pleasures of the glorified senses, or, rather, of the integral happiness of Heaven, we must be on our guard against several errors into which very good and even spiritual persons may easily fall.

∞

Heaven's happiness does not come chiefly from creatures

The first error consists in ignoring or making little of the Beatific Vision, after the resurrection, and letting our mind pass from creature to creature, gathering exquisite pleasures from each, until we practically make man's happiness in Heaven come almost exclusively from creatures. Some who hold this view have written books on the subject, in which they speak eloquently and even learnedly on the joys involved in the mutual recognition of friends and kindred, on the delights we shall enjoy in our social communion with the saints and angels, in the music that shall ravish our very souls, and other things of that nature. In a word, they maintain, as well as we do, that, in Heaven, man will enjoy every possible intellectual, moral, and sensible pleasure and that nothing will be wanting to make him perfectly happy in his whole being.

This view is certainly far from being gross or carnal. It may even, at first sight, appear not to differ from that which is taught by the Catholic Church. But, on closer examination, the difference becomes apparent. In this view, the Beatific Vision is either entirely ignored, or, if mentioned at all, it is explained so as to mean next to nothing — at least, it does not appear to add anything to the exquisite happiness already enjoyed in creatures. In this view, Heaven is really nothing more than a natural beatitude, such as might have been enjoyed even in this world if Adam had not sinned.

We must, therefore, be on our guard against any view of Heaven which would make its principal happiness come from creatures. We must always remember that no creature, either here or hereafter, can give perfect happiness to man. Wherefore, in our meditations on Heaven, we must beware of making its chief happiness consist in delightful music, in social communion with the saints, or in the pleasures enjoyed through the glorified senses, however pure and refined we may imagine them to be. This, then, is the first error to be avoided, and with much care; not only because it is untrue, but also because it lowers the beatitude of Heaven, which consists essentially in the vision, love, and enjoyment of God Himself.

∞

Creatures do contribute to heavenly happiness

The second error to be avoided consists in placing the whole happiness of man so completely and exclusively in the Beatific Vision, that neither the resurrection of the body with its glorious gifts, nor the communion of saints, nor heavenly music, nor any other creature, can increase the happiness already enjoyed by the soul in the possession of God. In this extreme and exclusive view of the Beatific Vision, man is so completely absorbed in God and so perfectly happy in Him, that the whole creation is to Him as if it were not. And if he were the only man ever created, or the only one in Heaven, his joys would be precisely the same as they would be if he were surrounded with angels, saints, and other creatures of God.

Those who hold such extreme views may be very holy persons, but their opinions are far from being in accordance with sound theology. They remind us of those unskillful guides who erroneously taught St. Teresa[54] that, in order to reach the most perfect contemplation in this world, we must raise our minds completely above every creature and that even the humanity of Christ Himself can be an impediment for those who have advanced far in spirituality: it hinders them from the most perfect contemplation. It is almost needless to add that she soon discovered this to be a very dangerous error, and, as may be

[54] St. Teresa of Avila (1515-1582), Spanish Carmelite nun and mystic.

seen in the twenty-second chapter of her autobiography, she expresses the deepest regret for having, even for a moment, entertained such an opinion. So will these persons of whom I speak discover their error, if they view the whole happiness of Heaven as it is taught by sound theology.

Let us, then, see what theology teaches on the resurrection of the body, as increasing the happiness of the blessed, and on the accidental beatitude which comes to man from creatures.

∞

You could not enjoy Heaven fully without your body

Theology teaches, first, that the resurrection is not a mere accidental glory, which may or may not be given to the just, but that it is an essential element of man's happiness.[55] The soul of Abraham, for instance, that is united to God in the Beatific Vision is not, properly speaking, Abraham himself, but only a part of him. In order, therefore, to be perfect according to its nature, his soul must again be clothed with its own body of real flesh and blood, so that Abraham may again be a living man and that God may be called, in the fullest sense of the word, "the God of the living."[56] Evidently the same must be said of every other soul now basking in the light of God's countenance.

We are not angels, but men. An angel is a superior being and of a different order from ours. He is a spirit and complete as such without a body. But the human soul, although a spirit too, is not perfect without a body, for, as such, it is only a part

[55] *Summa Theologica*, Suppl., Q. 75, art. 1.
[56] Matt. 22:32.

of the being called man. Besides, it is not the soul alone that is to enjoy the happiness of Heaven; it is the whole man. And as he is composed of both soul and body, it is necessary that the soul should again be clothed with its body, so that man may be placed in the enjoyment of Heaven's happiness in his whole being.

∞

The resurrection increases man's happiness

Theology teaches, in the second place, that the happiness of the blessed is increased by the resurrection, because the soul is enabled to receive new pleasures by its reunion with a glorified body. First, the human soul, which is not only intellectual, but also sensitive, receives those organs by which it is again enabled to exercise its imagination and other faculties of its emotional or sensitive nature, all of which are sources of great enjoyment.

Second, by the soul's reunion with the body, it is again empowered to receive pleasure through the glorified senses.

Third, the soul is made more perfect in all its operations by its reunion with a glorified body.[57] The human body as now constituted, or rather as injured by sin, does not, it is true, always perfect the soul in its operations; it rather impedes the soul, at least in many of them. Hence the wise man tells us that "the corruptible body is a load upon the soul, and the earthly habitation presseth down the mind that museth many things."[58] If, therefore, a glorified soul were reunited to such a body,

---

[57] *Summa Theologica*, Suppl., Q. 93, art. 1.
[58] Wisd. 9:15.

undoubtedly its operations would not be made more perfect than they are in its separate state. But it is not to be so. The soul is to be reunited to a glorified body, which will be entirely subject to the spirit, and will, in consequence, perfect all its intellectual operations, its moral affections, and every other act which, according to its nature, it can perform.

But, perhaps, some may say, "Will not the vision of God, at least, be lessened or obscured by the reunion of the soul with a material body?" It certainly will not. If the vision of the Divine Essence could be obscured by the risen body, then, as the Spanish Jesuit Theologian Francisco De Suarez wisely observes, the resurrection would be a punishment to the just, rather than a reward. Hence, he maintains that even the Beatific Vision is more perfect after the resurrection than it was before.

This becomes evident when we remember that the Beatific Vision consists of the three human acts of knowledge, love, and enjoyment of God. These acts are evidently more perfect after the resurrection, since the human soul acts more perfectly in union with a glorified body than when separated from it. It follows, then, that even the essential beatitude of the saints is both increased and perfected by the resurrection of the body. Let us now see what theology teaches about accidental glory.

∞

Happiness from creatures
will complete your happiness in Heaven
Theology teaches that accidental glory is any perfection of supernatural beatitude which comes to the blessed from any

object outside of the Beatific Vision, that is, from creatures. Thus, when our blessed Lord tells us that "there shall be joy in Heaven upon one sinner doing penance,"[59] He manifestly speaks of a new joy which comes to the blessed from an object outside of the Beatific Vision. So then, evidently, some of Heaven's joys do come from creatures, although, ultimately, we may say, they come from God.

In this world, we receive a portion of our light from the moon, but that light is still from the sun, because the moon has no light of its own. The moon is mere reflector or instrument by which, during the night, the sun conveys to us a portion of its light. So it is in Heaven. God is the only source of happiness and joy, and no creature is or can be a source of happiness independently of Him. But He can and does make use of creatures to adorn, perfect, and complete the happiness of the whole man.[60]

Nevertheless, although this accidental glory comes to the blessed from creatures, it is radically contained in the essential and is given with the essential as one reward, not as two. For there are not two beatitudes in Heaven. There is only one, which comprises both the essential and the accidental. It is true that we make a distinction between them, because one comes immediately from God, while the other comes from creatures. But it does not, in the least, follow that this accidental glory is of little use or to be despised. Considering the needs of our nature, which is not destroyed, but is perfected in Heaven, accidental glory is necessary to perfect and complete

[59] Luke 15:7.
[60] Francisco Suarez, *On Happiness*, disputation 11.

the blessedness of God's children and to gratify every rational craving of human nature.

Thus the crown of the virgins — who sing a canticle that no one else can sing, and who "follow the Lamb whithersoever He goes"[61] — is a mere accidental glory; and yet it is one so much prized that many have given life itself, amid the most cruel torments, in order to enjoy it. Thus again, our social communion with the saints, and the pure joys resulting therefrom, the meeting of our kindred and friends in Heaven, the ravishing music which resounds through the vaults of Heaven, the pleasures of the glorified senses — these and a thousand other joys are the accidental beatitude with which God perfects and completes the happiness of the whole man.

∞

You will remain active in mind and body

The third error which we shall now examine flows naturally from the mistaken and exclusive views which some persons take of the Beatific Vision. They imagine that the vision of God will so completely absorb and monopolize every faculty of man, that, practically, he will become motionless and inactive as a statue. There can be no greater mistake. It is true that our union with God, in the Beatific Vision, is happiness and joy greater than mortal man can conceive; but it by no means follows that it will hinder the free exercise of our mental faculties or the activities of our glorified bodies. Indeed, the very reverse will take place, for glory does not destroy nature, but perfects it.

[61] Rev. 14:4.

You will enjoy complete happiness

We are active by nature. Action, therefore, both of mind and body, is a law of our being, which cannot be changed, without radically changing, or rather destroying, our whole nature. As glory perfects our whole nature, instead of destroying it, it follows that in Heaven we shall be far more active than we can possibly be here below, for there all our powers will exist in their highest perfection.

Therefore, the intellect, elevated and strengthened by the light of glory, will continue to think and to contemplate the truth, for such is the natural action of the human intellect. Thus, also, the will, which is the loving power of the soul, shall continue forever to love, for its natural action is to love the good, the beautiful, and the perfect. The memory, also, will forever continue to recall the many graces received from God, thus keeping alive a deep sense of gratitude for His benefits, while the imagination will still continue to make to itself new and captivating pictures of beauty.

In the same way, the eye will continue to see material objects, for such is the natural action of that organ. The ear will continue to hear delightful sounds, and the whole body will continue to receive pleasurable sensations, and to perform all other actions which are natural to it, if we except those that belong merely to the natural life of man, for, as we have already seen, such actions are incompatible with a life and state of incorruption.

The soul of Jesus Christ enjoyed the Beatific Vision even while here on earth in mortal flesh. Was He, on that account, prevented from doing anything except contemplating the Divine Essence? He certainly was not. He labored and preached; He ate, drank, and slept; He visited His friends and did a thousand other things, without losing sight of the divine nature.[62]

Moreover, if the Beatific Vision is to overpower us, suspend our activities, and change us into statues, what could be the use of bestowing upon us the gift of agility? As we have seen, by that wonderful gift we shall be empowered to transport ourselves, with the rapidity of thought, to the most distant parts of God's universe. Is such a power to be given as a reward to God's children, and then rendered totally inactive and useless? We might as well say that although we shall have eyes, we shall not see. Wherefore, St. Thomas maintains that the blessed will go from place to place, according to their will, to exercise the power of agility which they have received, and to enjoy the beauty of God's creatures, which eminently reflect the divine wisdom.[63] And they shall not, on this account, lose anything of their essential happiness, which consists in the vision of God, for they will find Him everywhere present.

From all this sound theology it is evident that our union with God in the Beatific Vision, far from suspending or destroying the activities of our nature, will rather increase and perfect them. It will do so, first, by taking away from soul and body whatever now makes us sluggish; and, second, by adding to our existing faculties supernatural powers, which will give to our nature its highest degree of perfection and similitude to God, who is all activity.

We must be careful to remember all this; otherwise it will be impossible for us ever to understand how the saints can

---

[62] Cf. *Summa Theologica*, Suppl., Q. 82, art. 3.
[63] *Summa Theologica*, Suppl., Q. 84, art. 2.

possibly enjoy each other's society, rejoice at the conversion of sinners, listen to delightful music, enjoy the pleasures of the glorified senses, and otherwise exercise all the faculties and powers of their nature. The little glimpse of Heaven given in the Book of Revelation certainly does not represent the saints and angels as inactive statues. On the contrary, all is life and a wonderful activity.

We are now prepared to meditate upon the integral happiness of Heaven, which includes the resurrection of the body. This is the happiness which is to gratify every rational appetite of man.

Chapter Nine

You will enjoy
rest, peace, and love

We have examined the glorious gifts with which the risen body is clothed, and we have seen that it perfects the soul in all its operations and that the glorified senses are to contribute their share to the happiness of man. We shall now consider the happy life of the blessed in Heaven, including the resurrection.

But, remember, it is not a new life that is now to occupy our thoughts. It is a continuation of the same life that was begun the moment the vision of God flashed upon the soul. This heavenly life, which was enjoyed by the soul alone before the resurrection, is now enjoyed by the whole man, in its fullness and perfection.

If you dig in a dry and barren spot and happen to strike a vein of living water, it bubbles up, overflows, and moistens the surrounding earth, clothing it with beautiful verdure and smiling flowers.

So it is in the resurrection. The life which had been concentrated in the soul alone overflows to the body, giving to it life, beauty, and glory, and causing it to thrill with inexpressible pleasure. The Beatific Vision — which was the essential happiness of the soul before the resurrection — is now the essential happiness of man.

In our meditations on the life of Christ, we make ourselves present to the mysteries which we are contemplating. That is, we do not look upon them as past, but as actually taking place under our eyes. Thus we see Jesus lying in the manger. We see Him fleeing into Egypt and disputing with the doctors in the Temple. We see Him laboring, preaching, and dying upon the Cross.

Let us endeavor to do the same in our meditations on the life of the blessed.

Let us, then, transport ourselves in spirit to that great day which St. John saw, when a mighty angel, coming down from Heaven, stood upon the land and sea and, lifting up his hand on high, swore by Him who lives forever and ever that "time should be no more." Then, says St. John, "I saw the dead, great and small, standing in the presence of the throne, and the books were opened, and the dead were judged by those things which were written in the books. . . . And I heard a great voice from the throne, saying: Behold the tabernacle of God with men, and He will dwell with them, and they shall be His people; and God Himself shall be their God. And He that sat upon the throne said: Behold I make all things new."[64]

Here is a new order of things, in a new world — a world of beauty and perfection inconceivably greater than the one in which we now live. This is the world in which we are to live the life of the blessed. In this chapter, we shall examine five of its most prominent attributes.

[64] Rev. 10:5-6, 20:12, 21:3, 5.

∞
You will find perfect peace
First, it is a life of peace. When Jesus was born, the angels sang, "Glory to God in the highest, and on earth, peace to men of goodwill."[65] And when He rose from the dead, His first words to the Apostles were: "Peace be to you."[66] But, although the peace He wished and gave was great, it was not, and, in the existing order of things, could not be, perfect. For the Apostles still had to battle against the world, the Devil, and the flesh. But in Heaven that peace is perfect, because it flows immediately from the bosom of God Himself. Besides, none of those things which in this world disturb our peace can ever enter the kingdom of peace.

We now have perfect peace with God, of whose love for us we no longer doubt, as we may have often done when on earth. We also have peace with ourselves, for those unruly passions which formerly disturbed our peace no longer exist in our glorified bodies. We enjoy perfect peace with our neighbor, for conflicting interests, envies, and jealousies, which gave rise to dissensions and enmities, have not found and never will find, their way into Heaven. We also have peace from the assaults of the Devil, who no longer "goeth about like a roaring lion, seeking whom he may devour."[67] He has found no admittance into the kingdom of peace.

We also have peace from the troubles of our past life, because the sins which so often made us tremble are washed

[65] Luke 2:14.
[66] John 20:19.
[67] 1 Pet. 5:8.

away in the blood of Jesus and are therefore no longer a source of trouble. The remembrance of them, rather, intensifies our love for the God of mercy and therefore increases our happiness.

We now also have peace from the uncertainties of our future. That awful future was formerly shrouded in impenetrable darkness and often filled us with gloomy forebodings. But now the judgment is over, and we have heard the consoling sentence: "Come ye, blessed of my Father, possess the kingdom prepared for you, from the foundation of the world."[68] We now gaze undismayed into that bright outspread eternity, in which we see nothing that can ever disturb our peace. The wish and prayer of St. Paul expressed to the first Christians is now completely fulfilled in us: "And [may] the peace of God which surpasseth all understanding, keep your hearts and minds in Christ Jesus."[69]

This, then, is the first feature of heavenly life, and, as is evident, this peace is absolutely necessary to enjoy that life itself and whatever else of happiness is in store for the children of God.

∽

You will enjoy rest

The life of Heaven is one of rest. St. John says, "And I heard a voice from Heaven, saying to me, 'Write: Blessed are they that die in the Lord. From henceforth now, saith the Spirit, that they may rest from their labors.' "[70]

[68] Matt. 25:34.
[69] Phil. 4:7.
[70] Rev. 14:13.

This is one of the most captivating features of heavenly life for the poor and for all others who labor much in this world. It also gives the most exquisite consolation to those who, on account of particular difficulties in the practice of virtue, have been fatigued and wearied almost unto death. Their whole spiritual life was one of continual labor and struggle, which at times so disheartened them that they felt strongly tempted to give up all further attempts at Christian perfection and to seek consolation and rest in the pleasures of this world.

Oh, how happy they now are! How grateful to God, who gave them the grace of final perseverance! They now enter into their rest, which shall nevermore be disturbed by toil or struggle. They now live a life of everlasting rest, although not one of inactivity.

For, as we have already seen, the life of Heaven is not one of inactivity, but one in which every energy of mind and body has its full and free action. As our life in Heaven is a participation of the life of God Himself, it must resemble that divine life, which, while it is ineffable rest, is ever active and operative in the creation, conservation, and government, not only of our own world, but also of those millions of other worlds that shine above our heads. Nevertheless, this continual exercise of our manifold faculties in Heaven does not, as in this world, generate fatigue, weariness, or disgust, but is the never-failing source of the highest and most rational pleasure.

What a consoling thought this is for the poor! In the world they labored much, and for scanty wages, which, in many instances, scarcely sufficed to keep them and their families from starvation. What a consolation also for persons who have devoted themselves to God in religious communities! By their vows they became poor for Christ's sake, and, like Him, they labored much. The wear and tear of the religious life deprived many of their health and strength, and yet they continued to labor as if they were in full vigor. Their day of rest has come at last. Their beloved Spouse has called them to Himself, that they might rest from their labors. The last words of the Church over them is a solemn prayer for that heavenly rest: "Eternal rest give unto them, O Lord. And let perpetual light shine upon them. May they rest in peace." Here is the end of all labor, struggle, and fatigue. Here is the beginning of a life of eternal, undisturbed repose.

∞

You will enjoy intellectual pleasures

The life of Heaven is also one of intellectual pleasure. We saw, in a former chapter, that man's intellect is filled to over-flowing with knowledge in the vision of God. We must now say a few words on the exquisite and pure pleasures which this knowledge produces.

Intellectual pleasures are, perhaps, the least generally known of all those which our nature can enjoy, for the great majority of the human race is made up of the poor, who are compelled to spend their lives in toiling for food and raiment. They are, in consequence, unable to develop their mental faculties and to enjoy high intellectual pleasures. And yet these pleasures are the highest, the most rational and satisfying which man can enjoy, because they are produced by the exercise of the intellect, which is the noblest faculty of the soul.

Some men of highly cultivated minds, such as theologians, philosophers, astronomers, mathematicians, and literary men, separate themselves from the world and its pleasures. They spend each day, and a great part of each night, in study, in the contemplation of the truth. They even forget to eat and drink and must be compelled by their friends to attend to the necessities of nature. Many of them have completely ruined their health by study; and some of them, such as Democritus the philosopher,[71] are reported to have even plucked out their eyes, so that they might have less distraction and thereby be enabled to meditate more profoundly upon the truths of their respective sciences. Now, I ask, is it in our nature to go through such terrible self-denials without compensation? Surely it is not. Therefore, the natural inference is that knowledge is a source of the most exquisite pleasures.

If it is so in this world, where the curse of sin has darkened the mind, and where knowledge is so limited and so mingled with error and doubt, what shall we say of those pleasures in Heaven? There the intellect of man receives a supernatural light; it is elevated far above itself by the light of glory; it is purified, strengthened, enlarged, and enabled to see God as He is in His very essence. It is enabled to contemplate, face-to-face, Him who is the first essential Truth. It gazes undazzled upon the first infinite beauty, wisdom, and goodness, from whom flow all limited wisdom, beauty, and goodness found in creatures.

Who can fathom the exquisite pleasures of the human intellect when it thus sees all truth as it is in itself? This is one of Heaven's secrets which we shall never fully understand, except when united to God in the Beatific Vision. Nevertheless,

[71] Democritus (c. 460-370 B.C.), the "laughing philosopher."

if ever we have enjoyed the pleasures produced by the perusal of a highly intellectual work, or felt the irresistible fascinations of some favorite science, we can, it seems, form some distant conception of intellectual pleasures in Heaven.

∞

You will enjoy enduring love

The life of Heaven is also one of love. As we have seen before, man cannot rest satisfied with the mere contemplation of truth and beauty, however pleasurable and satisfying such a contemplation may be. His will immediately seizes upon the truth and beauty presented by the intellect and loves with an intensity proportioned to the perfection of the object presented. Now, as God Himself, in His unveiled majesty, is the object presented to the will, and as He is the most perfect of all beings, it follows that the will loves in Heaven with an ardor of whose intensity we can form only a faint conception in our present state of trial.

There, at last, do the blessed fulfill to perfection the law which commands us to love God with our whole heart, with our whole soul, with all our strength, with all our mind, and our neighbor as ourselves.[72] Not only does each one of the blessed love, but he sees himself loved in return both by the Almighty and by every one of the saints. This makes Heaven a life of love, and, consequently, one of perfect happiness.

Think of this, you mortals, who crave human love. You desire to love and to be loved. Love is the sunshine of your lives. But, do what you will, it can never give you perfect happiness

---

[72] Cf. Mark 12:29-31.

here below, for when you have, at last, succeeded in possessing the object after which you so ardently sighed, you discover in it imperfections which you had not suspected before, and these lessen your happiness. But suppose, even, that you are of the few who are as happy as they expected to be. How long will your blessedness last? A few years, at most. Then, death, with a merciless hand, tears away from you the objects of your love. Is not this the end of all earthly happiness?

Look up to Heaven, and see there the blessed in the presence of God. They are as happy today in their love as they were hundreds of years ago; and when millions of ages have rolled by, they shall still possess the object of their love, which is the eternal God. Thus the blessed live a life of love, and, consequently, one of perfect happiness.

∞

Your enjoyment will be undisturbed

The life of Heaven is, moreover, one of perfect enjoyment. In this world, there can be no perfect and lasting enjoyment. This is not only because creatures do not have the power of giving perfect happiness, but also because our powers of enjoyment are imperfect in themselves, and because our hearts swarm with ungoverned passions, which spread the gall of bitterness over our joys.

How many thousands are there for whom fortune smiles in vain! How many are there, who, although surrounded with untold wealth, are nevertheless more wretched than tattered beggars. One, for instance, is always suffering from bad health, and hence, he cannot enjoy the pleasures which fortune has placed within his reach. Another is not only wealthy, but is, moreover, elevated to some honorable position, and one would think he must enjoy the honors with which he is surrounded; but there is in his heart an ungoverned passion, which, like a cankerworm, eats away his joys one by one.

Holy Scripture gives us a striking instance of this in the person of Haman. He had been highly exalted by King Assuerus, and the servants of the king bent the knee before him and worshiped him, but "Mardochai did not bend the knee or worship him."[73] This apparent slight so wounded the pride of Haman that he could enjoy neither peace nor happiness so long as Mardochai, the Jew, sat at the king's gate. Listen to his own confession: "He called together his friends and Zares his wife, and he declared to them the greatness of his riches, and the multitude of his children, and with how great glory the king had advanced him above all his princes and servants. And after this, he said, 'Queen Esther also hath invited no other to the banquet with the king, but me; and with her I am also to dine tomorrow with the king. And whereas I have all these things, I think I have nothing, so long as I see Mardochai, the Jew, sitting at the king's gate.' "[74]

What a revelation this is! How little it takes to destroy our powers of enjoyment! It is only a small worm that eats away the very core of the most delicious fruit, leaving it tasteless and rotten.

In Heaven only shall we live a life of perfect enjoyment, not merely because all the objects of happiness exist there in their highest perfection, but because we shall also be made

[73] Esther 3:2
[74] Esther 5:10-13

perfect by our union with God. "We shall be like Him, because we shall see Him as He is." Wherefore, no inordinate passion will ever lurk in our heart and spread bitterness over our joys. No torturing disease will ever enervate or prostrate the energies of our glorified bodies and render them incapable of enjoyment. All the powers of enjoyment which belong to the glorified state will ever remain fresh and unimpaired. It follows from this that our life in Heaven will be one of continued, undisturbed enjoyment of God Himself, of the society of the saints, and of all other creatures that He has prepared to perfect and complete the beatitude of man.

Chapter Ten

∞

Your senses will be glorified

The life of Heaven is also one of pleasure through the glorified senses. These pleasures, as well as those of the Beatific Vision, are certainly beyond our comprehension. Still, we may form an idea of them by reflecting on the exquisite delights which reach our soul through our senses in our present state of imperfection. These are so fascinating that the world runs wild with their intoxication. What must they be in Heaven, where everything is perfect? For, in that world of God's magnificence, both the senses and their respective objects exist in their highest perfection, which is far from being the case here below.

Now, give free scope to your imagination. Let it roam among the blessed and flutter from creature to creature. Build up all you can of pure pleasure, and you will never reach more than the faintest shadow of the reality. Gaze upon the glorious body of Jesus Christ, the most perfect and lovely that ever came from the hand of God; it is the very sun that gives beauty to the whole of Heaven. Then contemplate the transcendent beauty of the Immaculate Mother, who, next to Jesus, is clothed with the greatest glory. Feast your eyes upon that countless multitude of saints. They are all beautiful, because they have all risen with a body glorified after the likeness of Christ's glorious body. Each one has a beauty and perfection of his own, according to his merits; and the very lowest is clothed with a loveliness far superior to anything ever seen in this world.

If there is a rush to see beautiful objects, grand and sublime sights, magnificent scenery, and the works of art, on account of the intense pleasure enjoyed through the sense of sight, what shall we say of the exquisite pleasures in store for that sense in Heaven?

Then again, reflect on how very captivating, soothing, and enlivening music is. The ear revels in it and pours into the soul torrents of harmony, which make the soul for the time forget the outer world altogether. So captivating is the music, that hours pass by unheeded, and the soul would almost fancy it is the echoes of angels' voices it hears. What, then, must heavenly harmony be, if our imperfect music is so delightful?

Think, also, how exquisitely the odors of flowers, incense, and all manner of perfumery produce a soothing effect upon man, banishing cares and infusing a new life into him. What must those pleasures be in Heaven?

We have already seen that, in Heaven, there is to be neither eating nor drinking, as we now understand these two actions. But this does not mean that the sense of taste is not to be gratified. It most certainly will be, although not by corruptible objects, as in this world. The same must be said of the sense of touch or feeling, which is diffused over the whole body.

The five senses of the human body are not mere accidental ornaments, which may or may not exist; they are essential to the integrity of its nature. Thus a blind man or a deaf and dumb man is not a perfect man, because he lacks something which is essential to the integrity of his nature. Now, as glory does not destroy the nature of the body, but perfects it, it follows that all the blessed must rise with their five senses in their full perfection. And as their perfection consists in their activity and power of receiving impressions from external objects, and conveying them to the soul, it is evident that the senses must remain active in Heaven and have suitable objects to act upon. This is precisely what we learn from St. Thomas Aquinas, who maintains that the glory of the body does not destroy its nature, but perfects it, and even preserves the very color that is natural to it.[75] He maintains, moreover, that every power or faculty is more perfect when acting upon its proper object, than it is when inactive; and, as human nature will reach its highest degree of perfection in Heaven, it follows that every sense will there act according to its nature.[76]

∞

Your whole being will enjoy Heaven

According to this doctrine, not one sense of the human body is either dead, inactive, or excluded from enjoyment in Heaven. And why should any one of them be excluded? Why should the sight, or the hearing, or even the sense of smell, be rewarded, rather than the taste, or the sense of touch? Certainly no valid reason can be given.

Theologians teach that, in Hell every sense of the human body shall have its own peculiar punishment, and that the sense of feeling, especially, shall be tortured, because, in most cases, it is principally in that sense that the reprobate have

[75] *Summa Theologica*, Suppl., Q. 85, art. 1.
[76] *Summa Theologica*, Suppl., Q. 82, art. 4.

most offended God. Surely we must not imagine that God is more severe in punishing the wicked than He is good and liberal in rewarding the just.

Now, is it not precisely in the senses of taste and feeling that the saints have suffered most for God? Look at that countless multitude of martyrs. Many were starved to death; others were scourged until they died under the torture; others were torn by the wild beasts; others were crucified; others were burned with a slow fire; while others were tortured for days together in every limb and sense, with all the ingenuity and appliances that the most refined cruelty could devise.

Then again, look at that countless multitude of confessors, virgins, and others, who, in the practice of virtue, became their own executioners. They suffered inconceivably by frequent and long fasts, by coarseness of diet, by wearing hair shirts, and by otherwise torturing their flesh. And now, shall these senses go unrewarded in the blessed, while they are terribly punished in the reprobate? Certainly not.

All that we can say is that, at present, we do not know how all this is to be realized; but as the whole man in all his senses has served God, and suffered for Him, it is only just that he should be rewarded in his whole being, which includes every sense of the body, as well as every faculty of the soul.

∞

You will enjoy pleasures without fear of shame
Hence, in our meditations on Heaven, we must let the pleasures of the glorified senses enter as an integral element of man's happiness. We must contemplate these pleasures as seriously as we do the pain of sense in the reprobate, only avoiding

the introduction of anything gross or carnal and therefore repugnant to a state of incorruption. Hence we must avoid introducing eating, drinking, sleep, or anything else which, by its very nature, belongs to the animal life of man.

We must also banish from our ideas of Heaven all the carnal pleasures of this world, as they are now understood. Our blessed Lord Himself told the Jews, who believed such pleasures to exist in Heaven: "You err, not knowing the Scriptures, nor the power of God. For, in the resurrection, they shall neither marry nor be married, but shall be as the angels of God in Heaven."[77] All such pleasures, which were intended only for this world of imperfection, will be replaced by others of a superior order and suited to our spiritualized bodies.

So, then, we see that the life of Heaven is one of sensible pleasure through the glorified senses, as well as one of exquisite mental and moral enjoyment in the Beatific Vision. These sensible pleasures have, moreover, a peculiar characteristic, which the pleasures of sense do not have in our present state of imperfection. In Heaven, the blessed can enjoy them all without fear, for none of them are forbidden, and, consequently, they can never be followed by bitter remorse or shame. Neither have they, as in this world, a tendency to darken the mind and turn the heart away from God. They will rather intensify our love for Him, who is the Author of our exceeding blessedness, whether it comes immediately from Himself, or partly from the beautiful creatures He has prepared to complete the happiness of His beloved children.

[77] Cf. Mark 12:24-25.

∞

Chapter Eleven

You will enjoy the company of others

The life of Heaven is also one of pure social joys. Among all the joys outside of the Beatific Vision, there are certainly none so sweet as those which arise from our social communion with the blessed. We are social beings by nature. Our highest and best powers are framed for society, and so we are never in our normal state except when in communion with our fellowmen.

Hence, all men love society, if we except the misanthrope, who is a moral monster. He has unfortunately developed in his heart some of the worst passions of our fallen nature, and they have built an element of Hell in his heart. For in that godless and hopeless region, there is no love either for God or neighbor, and, therefore, social joys can have no existence therein.

With the exception of a few persons of this kind, all men love society. Even the lonely hermit loves it. But he sees in society dangers to his soul, and he cuts himself off from it in this world, so that he may enjoy it in the next, where it shall have lost its dangerous element.

Social communion with our fellow beings affords us some of our purest joys in this world, yet they are not, and never can be, perfect. They are roses with cruel thorns that wound and make us bleed, almost as often as they delight us with their delicious perfumes.

How often does it happen that we go into society with a light heart and return home sad and heavy? And why is this so? It is because our heart has been wounded, perhaps crushed, by some wicked insinuation, or some unkind interpretation of an action performed with the best of intentions on our part. Even our holiest actions are criticized, and unworthy motives, which never entered our minds, are attributed to us. Then again, those whom we had considered our best friends may betray us and reveal to a cold and cruel world the secrets which, in our simplicity, we had confided to them.

In a word, if social communion with our fellow creatures is often the source of pure joys, it is not unfrequently the occasion of our keenest sufferings. And why? Because, in our present state of imperfection, we are sinful and selfish, because we allow ourselves to act toward others through jealousy, envy, natural aversion, and other ungoverned passions of our fallen nature. We do not love all men, and all men do not love us. We see many defects in others, which make them unamiable, and others see as many defects in us, which make their love for us almost an impossibility. Wherefore, so long as we live in the flesh, our social joys must always be mingled with a certain amount of bitterness.

Let us now raise our eyes to our heavenly home and there contemplate a life of the purest and most perfect social pleasures. There, neither selfishness, nor uncharitableness, nor any unruly passion can exist, and, consequently, our social joys will never be mingled with the gall of bitterness. Putting aside, for a moment, all the shortcomings and imperfections that mar our social joys in this world, let us look at their bright side only and see what it is that makes our social communion with others a pleasure. This will be as a mirror in which we shall behold some faint reflections of social joys as they exist in Heaven.

What are the personal attributes or qualities in others that make our social communion with them a pleasure? They may be reduced to six, which really include all others that could be mentioned. These are virtue, learning, beauty, refinement, mutual love, and the ties of kindred. We shall say a few words on each of these.

∽

Holiness will enhance your social joys

Virtue is the attribute which gives us our highest similitude to God, and it is this also which imparts to us some of the purest social pleasures we enjoy on earth. Purity of life, or at least the absence of gross vices, is a condition without which we can enjoy no one's society, unless we ourselves are depraved. Neither beauty, nor learning, nor any other endowment, can replace virtue, while it alone can, to a great extent, supply all other deficiencies. Hence it is that when depraved persons are in the society of the good, they feel compelled to be guarded in their words and actions. They must put on an exterior appearance, at least, of virtue, well knowing that otherwise their presence would be extremely offensive and calculated to mar the pleasures of others.

When we meet with one who is evidently a man of God, one whose every word is instinct with the spirit of God, whose whole exterior betokens the intimate union of his soul with

The Happiness of Heaven

God, in whose very countenance the beauty of angelical purity shines forth, we deem it a happiness to spend a few moments in his society. The pleasures enjoyed in his company are not only exquisite — they are also sanctifying. If that is so in this world, where all holiness is imperfect, what shall we say of the pleasures of heavenly society?

Holiness is an essential attribute of every inhabitant of Heaven. They are all pure, for none but the pure can see God. They are all made partakers of the divine nature in a far higher degree than is attainable in this world, and, consequently, they are all clothed with the spotless purity of God Himself. Not only are they all pure, but they are, moreover, totally free from those natural defects of character which, in this world, make many holy persons unamiable and even repulsive. As nature is not destroyed, but is perfected, by glory, our natural character will not be destroyed by our union with God. But whatever is faulty in it, or offensive to others, will disappear, leaving it amiable and perfect in its own kind. Hence, our social communion with the saints will ever be the source of the purest pleasures.

∞

Learning is a source of pleasure

Learning, in those with whom we associate, is another source of pleasure. We can sit for hours listening to the interesting conversation of a learned man, even if he lacks virtue and only wears its exterior appearance. In such a man's society, we drink in, as it were, torrents of pleasures, which are among the most rational we can enjoy in this world. If these pleasures are so exquisite here below, where, after all, the wisest know so little, what shall we say of those same pleasures in Heaven? There all are learned, all are filled with knowledge, although all do not possess it in the same degree. Nevertheless, each one's knowledge will be a source of pleasure to others.

∞

You will enjoy great beauty and refinement

Personal beauty is also a source of pleasure in this world. Everyone knows that perfect personal beauty sweetly but powerfully draws men to itself, and that one endowed with it gives far greater pleasure than another who does not possess this attribute. It is in Heaven, and there only, that everyone will possess the attribute of beauty in its fullest perfection. For there the soul is clothed with the beauty of God Himself, which He communicates to it in the Beatific Vision, and the whole body is beautified and glorified after the likeness of Christ's glorious body. Every saint is, therefore, clothed with a loveliness far superior to anything we ever can see on earth. If, then, it is so great a pleasure to associate with persons who possess the natural and perishable beauty of this world, what pleasure shall come from our communion with persons who are clothed with the beauty of God Himself!

Refinement is another attribute which makes our social communion with others pleasurable. A great personal beauty that might at first attract others to itself would soon repel and even disgust them, should they perceive in its possessor unpolished manners, coarseness, and stupidity. A cultivated intellect, refined feelings, and elegant manners are necessary to adorn personal beauty and make it a source of pleasure to those who are attracted by it. It is very certain that in Heaven, where our whole nature is to be elevated and perfected, this refinement of mind and heart, as well as the elegance of personal bearing which flows from both, will exist in its highest perfection and ever be the source of exquisite pleasures in our social communion with the blessed.

∞

You will love and be loved perfectly

Another source of social joys is mutual love. The four personal attributes we have been considering make up an amiable character — that is, one which we love spontaneously and whose love we are certain to have in return for ours. It is this love which crowns and perfects a character of this kind and produces a very large share of the pure pleasures we enjoy in the society of such persons. But, however pure human love may be, even when elevated by grace to the virtue of charity, it never can produce unalloyed social pleasures, because it never reaches its full perfection in this world.

It is in Heaven only that charity is perfect. There we shall love everyone with a most tender charity and see ourselves loved as tenderly and as purely in return. Our charity will be mutual, and, therefore, our communion with the blessed will produce joys and pleasures second only to the unspeakable happiness of the Beatific Vision.

Meditate well, Christian soul, on these exquisite delights. Think what an unspeakable pleasure this mutual and perfect charity must be to the inhabitants of Heaven. For any one of us, that feature alone would almost change this cold world into a heaven.

You will enjoy the company of others

Suppose you were able to say, with truth, "Every one of my acquaintances loves me with the purest charity; and every stranger who is introduced to me loves me immediately with the purest affection. I have no enemies — no, not one. No one is ever envious or jealous of me. No one ever says an unkind word of me, nor does anyone have even an unkind thought about me. All seem to take a singular pleasure in speaking well of me and in doing me all manner of kind services; and, in return, I sincerely love all and take a singular delight in doing good to all." Surely, such language never was spoken by anyone in this world of imperfection. If, therefore, you could speak it with truth, you would have reached a blessedness which neither our blessed Lord nor any of His saints ever reached on earth. Everyone would look upon you — and with reason — as the most highly favored person who ever lived in this world.

Now, this is precisely the blessedness which awaits us in our heavenly home. There we shall love everyone with the most perfect charity, and everyone will return our love. There we shall have no enemies: no one to think uncharitably of us, no one to criticize our sayings and conduct, no one to spread reports injurious to our character, no one to put an unfavorable construction upon our most innocent actions. "God is charity,"[78] and because "we shall be like Him because we shall see Him as He is," it follows that we, too, shall possess that divine charity, in a far higher degree than is attainable here below. Our social communion with the blessed will, therefore, ever be the source of the purest and sweetest joy.

[78] 1 John 4:8.

∞

You will be reunited with your loved ones

Besides the things already enumerated, there is one more which is to be the source of still greater joy. And what may that be? It is the meeting, in Heaven, of those whom we loved so well here because they were bound to us by the sacred ties of kinship or of true friendship. It is the meeting of parent and child, of husband and wife, of brother and sister, of relatives and friends with whom we were united by the bonds of the purest love. As glory does not destroy our nature, neither does it destroy our natural virtues, but it perfects them. Hence, we shall take along with us our natural love for our relatives and friends.

Thus, Jesus Christ, our model, now loves His blessed Mother with the natural love of a dutiful son. He loves her, not only because she is pure and holy, but also because she is His own Mother. The elevation of His human nature above everything that is not God, has neither destroyed nor diminished in Him that natural love which every child has for his mother. Thus, again, Mary now loves Jesus most tenderly, not only because He is her God, but also because He is her own Son, flesh of her flesh, and bone of her bone.[79] Her elevation to the highest glory, after that of Jesus, has neither destroyed nor diminished in her the natural love which every mother has for her child. If anything, it has made her love more ardent even than it was in this world.

So we, also, shall enter Heaven with the natural love we now have for our kindred and friends, but in us it will be

---

[79] Cf. Gen. 2:23.

purified from everything inordinate or imperfect. What a delight that meeting must be for the blessed! We can even now
form some faint idea of that heavenly joy by reflecting on what
takes place when a beloved father returns home from a long
and perilous voyage, or from some cruel war, where he had
been daily exposed to captivity and death. What outbursts of
gladness among the members of his family! How happy they
are to see him and embrace him!

If these joys are so great in this world, imagine what they
must be in Heaven — especially since there they are coupled
with the thought that there is no more separation! No more
separation, what delightful music there is in those words!
Death shall be no more, and therefore we shall never again be
torn away from the society of our kindred and friends.

However, it seems to me that I hear you say, "There is no
difficulty in believing that the meeting of our own in Heaven is
an unspeakable joy, but suppose we do not meet them there —
what then? Suppose that, on entering Heaven, we learn that
our father, our mother, or some other loved one is lost forever.
Shall we still be happy? Will there not be in such a case an essential element wanting to complete our happiness?" We shall
devote the next chapter to answering this difficulty, which is a
lifelong torture to many a pious mind.

Chapter Twelve

∞

You will be happy
with God's judgments

Will the knowledge that some of our own are lost mar our happiness in Heaven? This is a difficult question to answer satisfactorily, on account of our instinctive feelings of natural affection, which arise and, like a mist, obscure our judgment. Nevertheless, the difficulty is much lessened, and even entirely removed from some minds, at least, by the following considerations.

Our happiness, even in this world, does not depend on the happiness of those who are bound to us by the ties of kinship or of friendship. This is especially the case when their unhappiness proceeds from their own misdeeds. In such a case, we even inflict the punishment ourselves, and we regard it as just for them to suffer according to their deserts.

Thus, a father may banish from the paternal roof a son or a daughter who has committed a deed that has brought disgrace upon the family. And what is more, the whole family ratifies the terrible sentence. The presence and happiness of that brother or sister is not strictly necessary for the family's own happiness.

If such is the case in this world, why not in Heaven?

The Happiness of Heaven

∞

You will judge according to God's justice

In Heaven, we shall be like God, because "we shall see Him as He is." This moral transformation, as we have already seen, is the work of the Beatific Vision. By that glorious vision, and consequent union with God, we shall participate in all the attributes of God which are communicable to a rational nature. One of these attributes is justice — that is, the power of judging as God does, without passion, prejudice, or any of those motives which, in this world, render our judgments rash, unjust, or partial. Not only shall we be clothed with the power of judging justly, but with it we shall have a desire that everyone be rewarded or punished according to his works; and we shall rest perfectly satisfied to see the just sentence carried into effect.

Even now we possess that attribute, as well as others which make us the living images of the Most High. But it is far from being perfect, because our feelings, private interests, and passions warp our judgments and even reverse them after we have pronounced a just sentence.

Suppose, for instance, you hear of a man who has committed a premeditated murder. You are horrified at the atrocious deed, and, without a moment's hesitation, you pronounce in your heart that man's sentence. Your judgment is that he must die on the scaffold, or at least that he be deprived of liberty and condemned to hard labor for the remainder of his days. But you have scarcely pronounced this just sentence when you discover that the murderer is your own father!

What a change this one circumstance will bring about in your judgment! If you are of an affectionate nature, you will do

You will be happy with God's judgments

all in your power to find circumstances that may lessen or pal-
liate his guilt. Perhaps you may even succeed in making him
appear, in your eyes, wholly innocent, and thus your first judgment is entirely reversed. What is it that has changed your
first judgment? Is it your deep sense of justice? Not at all.
Your instinctive feelings of love have blinded you and made it
impossible for you to judge his case fairly and on its own
merits.

But, again, if you are not of an affectionate nature, you may
be so transported with rage at your father's crime that you can
find no punishment severe enough for him. And why is this
so? Because you see yourself and your family forever disgraced.
You feel your cheek burning with shame, and, in your desire
for revenge, you heap maledictions upon your unfortunate father's head. Here, again, your judgment is wrong, because it is
dictated by an unmanly desire for revenge. So, in either case,
you are unable to judge fairly and to pronounce a just sentence, simply because the criminal is your own father.

Now, it is very certain that none of these prejudices or passions, which now interfere so much with our judgments, will
follow us into Heaven. There, clothed with the justice and
sanctity of God Himself, we shall judge as He does, without
passion or prejudice. And the fact that the criminal is our own
father, or mother, or other loved one will neither influence
nor reverse our judgments. I do not mean to say that we shall
actually sit in judgment and pronounce the sentence of con-
demnation against our own kindred; but I do mean that, seeing the justice and fairness of God's judgments, we shall
readily acquiesce therein, and ratify them, and rest satisfied to
see all suffer according to their deserts.

A third consideration is taken from the nature of love. When love for anyone has taken full possession of our soul, it so completely changes us that we forget our own private interests and embrace his cause, his interests, as if they were our own. Henceforth, our will is so absorbed by his, that we seem no longer to possess any will of our own.

Holy Scripture gives us a striking instance of this transforming power of love in the friendship of Jonathan for David. According to the expression of Holy Scripture, "The soul of Jonathan was knit with the soul of David, and Jonathan loved him as his own soul."[80] David had slain the famous Goliath, and when the Jewish army was returning home in triumph, the women sang, "Saul slew his thousands, and David his ten thousands."[81] King Saul was filled with anger and envy on hearing David praised more than himself; and, from that day, he hated David and did all in his power to destroy him. His son Jonathan, who loved David as his own soul, left nothing undone to save his friend. He watched everything his father said or did, discovered all his plans against David, and then would go into the forest, at his own peril, and warn his friend of approaching danger.[82]

And Jonathan did more: he forgot, or gave up, all his own private interests, and embraced those of David. For, being the son of a king, he had the presumptive right to succeed his father upon the throne, but, instead of himself, he wanted David to reign in his father's place. He did even more: he embraced a

[80] 1 Kings 18:1 (RSV = 1 Sam. 18:1).
[81] 1 Kings 18:7 (RSV = 1 Sam. 18:7).
[82] 1 Kings 20 (RSV = 1 Sam. 20).

line of conduct entirely opposed to the temporal interests of his own father, and he thus materially aided in placing David upon the throne of Israel.

This is a striking instance of the wonderful transforming power of love. Now, if human love has such a power in this world, what shall we say of the power of divine love in Heaven! There we shall see God as He is, and that vision will kindle in us a love far greater than we ever had, or could have, for anyone in this world. We shall, therefore, spontaneously espouse God's cause and embrace His interests. We shall love all that He loves, and we shall find it impossible to love those whom He does not and cannot love.

Hence, we shall never love Lucifer, or any of those fallen spirits who sided with him in his rebellion against God and became demons on that account. Nor shall we ever love any of those who lived a bad life, stubbornly persisted in their sins, and died at enmity with God. If we can no longer love them, we shall certainly not lose a single degree of our happiness on finding that they are not in Heaven.

∞

Absence of loved ones will not mar your happiness

The fourth and last consideration I place before you is that, if the salvation of all their own were necessary for the happiness of the blessed, it might follow that very few, if any, could be happy in Heaven. For it may be that there are only very few, if any, among the blessed, who see every member of their family and all their relatives and friends around them in the abode of bliss. It would follow, too, that even the angels are unhappy, for, before the rebellion of Lucifer and his accomplices, they certainly loved each other, and probably with more perfection and intensity than we ever loved anyone in this world. And now they see a vast multitude of their former friends and associates in endless misery. Are they unhappy on that account? Certainly not.

It is evident, then, that if we once admit that the salvation of our own is necessary for our individual happiness, we find ourselves compelled to admit also that Heaven is a place of sadness and mourning, since there are many there who are not surrounded by those whom they loved in this world. The absurdity which necessarily follows from such an admission is, by itself, a sufficient answer to the difficulty.

Remember that, in Heaven, "we shall be like God, because we shall see Him as He is." We shall, therefore, be like God in beatitude. Now, is God made unhappy because some of His creatures have refused Him obedience and love, and have, in consequence, lost themselves forever? Certainly not. And did He ever love those same creatures as much as we love father, or mother, brother, sister, or friend? Certainly He did. His love for them was so great, that ours, however pure and ardent, sinks into insignificance when compared with His. Did we ever offer ourselves to suffer every imaginable indignity and torture for our kindred?

God alone is capable of so great a love. He assumed our nature, and in it He suffered more than the human mind can conceive. Look at Him in the garden, oppressed and overpowered with an agony of sorrow. Follow Him through the different stages of His bitter Passion. Contemplate that cruel scourging, the crowning with thorns, the filthy spittle covering His sacred face, and the other insults and indignities heaped upon Him. Follow Him to Mount Calvary; see Him nailed upon an infamous gibbet, suffering every torture of mind and body to His very last breath.

And why did He undergo all this? Because He loved us. And now, are all those, whom He loved so well, and for whom He suffered so much, around the throne of His glory in Heaven? They certainly are not. If, then, His happiness is not marred by the loss of those whom He loved so much, neither shall ours be, if we find that some of our own are lost. We shall be like Him in beatitude, "because we shall see Him as He is."

∞

Lead others to holiness in this life

In the meantime, do all in your power to instill principles of virtue into your children if you are a parent or into your pupils, if you are a teacher, or into any over whom you have authority. See that none of them is lost through your own fault. For if there is one thing above all others that is difficult to understand, it is how fathers and mothers can be happy in Heaven when they see their own children lost through their own negligence or bad example. Again, how can teachers, guardians, and pastors of souls be happy in Heaven when they see those committed to their care ruined forever through their negligence? Again, how can those men be happy who have seduced others from the path of virtue, by immoral discourses, bad books, and evil actions?

These certainly are hard things to understand, and still we must believe that all who enter Heaven are happy. We must believe, moreover, that careless and even bad parents, negligent teachers, seducers of the innocent, and writers of bad books, will eventually be admitted into Heaven if they die truly repentant. We must believe, moreover, that all such persons will be happy in Heaven, no matter how many they have ruined, for the simple reason that no unhappiness can ever find its way into the abode of bliss.

Chapter Thirteen

∞

The light of glory will enable you to see God

Having, in the foregoing chapters, endeavored to form an idea of Heaven's happiness, we must now endeavor to understand something of the different degrees in which each one of the blessed enjoys that unspeakable beatitude.

It is an article of Faith that except for the very young every-one in Heaven is rewarded according to his own personal mer-its acquired in this life by the assistance of God's grace. Those who have lived long enough to be responsible for their deeds, besides being admitted there in virtue of their adoption as children of God by means of Baptism, are, moreover, rewarded according to their own personal merits.

But I hear you ask, "Does not the happiness of Heaven con-sist in the Beatific Vision?" Undoubtedly it does. "And is the little boy who dies before he can make an act of faith or of charity admitted to that glorious vision as well as the apostle and the martyr?" Certainly he is. "And the little girl who dies before reaching the age of discretion — is she, too, admitted to the vision of God, as well as the Sister of Charity, the nun, and others who spend their lives in teaching the ignorant and ministering to the poor?" Undoubtedly she is. "And the murderer, who dies on the scaffold after making an act of perfect contrition — is he, too, eventually admitted to the vision and possession of God?" Yes, he, too, will see God face-to-face, and be made happy by that glorious vision.

"Well, then, if all see and possess God, how can there be a difference in the happiness of the saints? Are they not all equally happy?" This is the question we are now to answer, by examining the meaning and the nature of the light of glory. This examination will make it evident, that, although all see God, yet no two of the blessed enjoy precisely the same degree or amount of happiness.

∞

The light of glory will
infuse your soul with power

Theologians define the light of glory to be, "a supernatural intellectual power infused into the soul, by which it is enabled to see God, which it never could do by its own unassisted natural powers."[83] It is called supernatural because it is not a natural talent or power of our nature, as the talent for poetry, music, painting, and others, all of which may be developed and highly improved by study. The light of glory is an elevation, expansion, or development of the mind, which comes directly from God and is, in no sense, the result of human endeavors, except insofar as it is the God-given reward for a holy life.

We shall understand better the meaning of the light of glory by an illustration.

[83] Francisco De Suarez, *On God*, ch. 14.

The light of glory

Let us suppose that you never could learn mathematics or astronomy. In spite of the most intense application, you never could master even the multiplication table, and when you gazed upon the heavens, you could never see there any more beauty and magnificence than does the untutored savage. But, suddenly, there is a flash of light from above, and your mind is enlightened far beyond its natural capacity, and you can see all the heavenly bodies as they are.

You now know their names, motions, distances, laws, and relations to each other and to the whole universe. Formerly, they appeared all alike, except the sun and the moon; but now, you see that no two of them are alike. Each one has its own size, velocity, beauty, and glory. You even soar far beyond the discoveries of science, and you gaze with delight upon millions of shining worlds, which the most powerful telescope has never reached, and never can reach. You can, moreover, in the twinkling of an eye, calculate with astonishing precision the day, the hour, the minute, yes, the very second, at which an eclipse will occur.

Gazing upon the heavens, which hitherto had given you so little satisfaction, now becomes the source of the most exquisite and rational pleasure. For you now see in these countless worlds so much beauty and magnificence, so delightful a harmony, that you can spend whole nights in the contemplation of the heavens.

In the supposition just made, you receive an accession or addition of intellectual power, which enables you to see clearly and to understand what was invisible and unintelligible to you before the flash enlightened you. The light of glory produces a similar effect upon the soul at its entrance into Heaven. Our mind, which is now unable to see God except "as through a glass, in a dark manner,"[84] is suddenly elevated in power and enabled to see God as He is, face-to-face, and to contemplate His divine beauty and His other perfections. Our individual mind is neither destroyed nor changed into another; it is only strengthened and elevated in power and capacity far beyond anything we could ever have reached by our own unassisted endeavors.

But we shall still better understand the meaning of the light of glory by contrasting it with the light of faith. What is faith? Faith is also a supernatural elevation of the mind, by which we are enabled to believe, as firmly as if we saw them, mysteries which are far above our comprehension. Faith is called supernatural because it is from God alone; no man bestows faith upon himself. Here, then, the light of faith and the light of glory resemble each other, inasmuch as they both come immediately from God and elevate man above himself. But they vastly differ in intensity, for by faith we see God imperfectly and unsatisfactorily, whereas by the light of glory we see God as He is in Himself. Faith, therefore, is as the first faint blush of the morning, while the light of glory is as the sun shining in its meridian splendor.

∞

Only through the light of glory
will you see God as He His
So, then, the light of glory is a supernatural addition to our mind, which enables it to cross the gulf between the Creator

[84] 1 Cor. 13:12.

and the creature. I say "gulf" because no created intelligence can by its own natural power see God as He is. Hence, neither St. Augustine, nor St. Thomas, nor any other giant intellect could see God as He is in Himself, any better than the man who never could learn his letters. It is in this sense that we must understand St. Paul when, speaking of God, he says, "Who alone hath immortality, and inhabiteth light inaccessible; whom no man hath seen, nor can see."[85] Evidently he means that no one can see God by the light of nature, for in another place he tells us that when that which is perfect has come, we shall see Him face-to-face.[86]

From all this it follows that all men are on a footing of perfect equality, so far as the power of seeing God is concerned. No one has that power in himself by nature, and no one can give it to himself or develop it by study, as we can other powers we have received in the natural order. It is as if we said that no man possesses the natural power to see through a stone wall or through the earth. Certainly all men are equal here, for the man whose eagle eye can recognize a friend at the distance of ten miles is no nearer to seeing through the earth than another whose sight is so bad that he can scarcely recognize his own father at a distance of a few steps.

So it is with seeing God. No man has the power in himself by nature, and, therefore, no one can develop it by study. Even the angels, who are so vastly superior to us in intelligence, could not see God as He is until they were elevated by the light of glory.

[85] 1 Tim. 6:16.
[86] 1 Cor. 13:10, 12.

The Happiness of Heaven

I have been particular in explaining and insisting upon these things, lest it might be imagined that men of highly cultivated minds, such as philosophers, theologians, poets, and the like, shall in virtue of their superior natural gifts, see God better and enjoy more of Heaven's happiness than the ignorant. They certainly shall not. God does not bestow a supernatural reward upon the natural gifts, or even upon the natural virtues which are to be found among pagans as well as among Christians. But He does reward the faith, hope, charity, and other supernatural virtues, which His children have practiced in this world.

∞

God bestows the light of glory according to merit

Hence, theology teaches that not even the angels, who are so superior to us, see God any better in virtue of their nobler and more perfect intellect. Thus, supposing an angel and a man to be equal in merit, they both receive the same amount of the light of glory; they both see God in the same degree of perfection; and both, therefore, enjoy the same degree of happiness. If we admit that the angel has a more perfect vision of God, on account of his more perfect natural intellect, then we must also admit that he enjoys a portion of supernatural beatitude exclusively in virtue of his natural powers, and not on account of his merits acquired by correspondence to divine grace. Evidently no such admission can be made, for Heaven is a supernatural reward of supernatural virtues, which have been practiced in this world under the influence of divine grace, and not a reward of natural endowments. If, then, no such doctrine can be admitted when the question is between angels and men, much less can it be admitted when there is question of superior natural intellect among men. Hence, the man who never learned his letters, either for want of natural talent or opportunity, shall undoubtedly see God as well as the philosopher, if he has led as good a life; and he shall see Him better, and enjoy more of Heaven's happiness, if he has lived a holier life.

Once more: the light of glory is a supernatural elevation of the mind, which enables man to see God as He is in Himself. It is given by God Himself to those who have lived a supernatural life of faith, hope, and charity. Moreover, it is given to each in proportion to his personal merits. It therefore becomes the measure of the degree of happiness which each one of the blessed enjoys in the vision of God.

Chapter Fourteen

You will enjoy your own
special happiness in Heaven

Having seen that the light of glory is the new power, or me-
dium, through which the blessed see and enjoy God, we must
now endeavor to understand how its different degrees of intensity become the source of vastly different degrees of happiness or enjoyment.

In order to understand how the different degrees of mental
elevation produce different degrees of happiness in the Beatific Vision, we must first examine what the different degrees
of enjoyment in the creatures that now surround us consist in.
This will be as a mirror, in which we can see faint, but true, reflections of the vast difference there is between the highest
and the lowest in Heaven.

In order for us to receive pleasure from creatures, it is not
enough to be surrounded with them, or even to possess them:
we must, moreover, be endowed with organs, or faculties,
through which we can receive and appropriate to ourselves
the pleasures that, according to their nature, they can give.
Therefore, a grand concert, which may pour the most exquisite pleasures into your soul, would give no pleasure at all to a
deaf man, because he lacks the receiving organ, and, hence, in

his regard, it is as if the pleasure-giving object did not even exist.

∞

Your earthly holiness will determine
your degree of happiness in Heaven

But this is not all. Not only does our pleasure depend upon the possession of receiving faculties, but the amount also, or degree, of that pleasure, depends upon the development and perfection of the same receiving organs and faculties. The more highly developed and cultivated they are, the more intense also will be the satisfaction and pleasure we shall receive from any given object; persons of inferior development will receive far less, although the object is the same for all. Let us make this evident by an illustration.

Take the thousands of persons who have read some literary work — say, for instance, the *Iliad* of Homer. They all had eyes, and all could read; they all encountered the whole book as completely as if it had been written for each one in particular; and, no doubt, they all received pleasure from the perusal of that beautiful poem. But, did they all receive the same amount of pleasure? They certainly did not. No two individuals ever received the same degree of pleasure or enjoyment from the perusal of that book. Each one received and appropriated to himself his own pleasure — which was great in proportion to the cultivation and elevation of his mind. Hence, while a superior and highly cultivated mind is entranced at the beauty and sublimity of some particular passage, an inferior one sees neither meaning nor beauty in it and perhaps even casts the book aside in disgust.

It would be easy to multiply illustrations, but this one is sufficient to show that the amount of pleasure we derive from the use of creatures depends upon the degree of development and perfection in our receiving faculties.

So it is in Heaven among the blessed. They all see and possess God. They all love and enjoy Him, but it by no means follows that they all enjoy the same amount of happiness from that blessed vision. And why is this so? Because each one sees and enjoys only in proportion to his individual development and elevation of mind — which is given to him by the light of glory. And, as that blessed light is given to each one according to his own personal merits, it follows that each one sees and enjoys God in proportion to the holiness of the life he lived while upon earth.

Hence, those who have practiced virtue in a heroic degree — who have sacrificed the pleasures of this world, honors, wealth, and even life itself, for God — possess the highest elevation of mind and, consequently, the highest degree of enjoyment. They possess the most intense and perfect vision of the Divine Essence. They soar higher and penetrate more deeply into the unfathomable being of God. They see more of the divine beauty, wisdom, goodness, and other perfections of God and partake more largely of the divine nature. In a word, their higher elevation of mind, by a more intense light of glory, is to them the source of the highest and most perfect enjoyment in the Beatific Vision — while persons of very inferior virtue, although perfectly happy too, enjoy a vastly inferior degree of blessedness.

But this is not all. We have seen, in a former chapter, that the Beatific Vision does not consist in merely gazing upon the surpassing beauty of God, and that the mere sight of Him, if it could be separated from the possession of Him, could not make anyone happy. Thus, the sight of God includes the possession of Him. It includes, moreover, the intense love to which that vision gives birth, as well as the consequent enjoyment of Him.

Now, it is evident that a more intense light of glory, or a greater elevation of the mind, inflames the soul with a more intense love for God. For, it reveals to the soul not only more of His surpassing beauty, but also more of His unspeakable love for the soul, and the soul's love for Him becomes greater in proportion. And the greater the love between the soul and God, the more perfect and complete is the union existing between them and, consequently, the higher is the happiness enjoyed by the soul.

Thus it is that all the blessed see, love, and enjoy God in the Beatific Vision. They are all perfectly happy, and yet, among the countless multitude of God's children, probably no two really enjoy the same degree of happiness. Each one enjoys according to the elevation of his mind, which he has deserved by the holiness of his life.

Not only is there a difference in the degrees of enjoyment, but there is also a gulf between the highest and the lowest in Heaven. It is, moreover, an impassable gulf, which the lowest can never cross so as to reach the highest happiness of Heaven. It would be far easier for the lowest and most uncouth servant-maid in a king's palace to reach the dignity and glory of a queen than it is for the lowest in Heaven to reach the most intimate degree of union with God. Each one is happy in the degree and sphere which his life has deserved for him, but in that degree each one will and must remain forever.

∽

You can aspire to a high
degree of glory in Heaven

I trust that you now understand something of the different degrees of happiness in Heaven and that, at the same time, you are filled with a holy ambition to reach a high degree of union with God. If so, thank God. For a high degree of glory in Heaven is within the reach of us all, however poor, ignorant, or insignificant we may be here below.

Heaven is not as this world, where the mere accident of birth, or the smile of fortune, instead of moral worth, generally determines a man's position in society, as well as the amount of natural happiness he shall enjoy. Hence, no poor girl ever imagines that, if she is very virtuous, some great king will eventually espouse her and elevate her to the dignity and glory of a queen. No poor boy ever believes that, if he behaves well, and obeys the laws of the land as a good citizen, the king will, in consequence, eventually adopt him as one of his sons and bestow upon him the honors and pleasures which may be enjoyed by royal children.

But even supposing that such wild dreams could be realized in this world, these ignorant and uncouth people could not be made happy in their elevated position. And why? Because the king, who has the power to give palaces, wealth, magnificent dresses, and tables loaded with every imaginable luxury, has not the power to bestow the elevation of mind, polish of manners, and other graces which befit queens and royal children. Hence, they would feel out of place and be unable to enjoy the happiness to which they have been elevated. Besides, they would see themselves despised and even ridiculed by those whose birth and education have fitted them for high society. The mere fact, therefore, of their elevation to high honors would not clothe them with the personal qualities which are necessary to enjoy the highest honors and pleasures of this world.

How different all this is, when there is question of Heaven! For, however poor and ignorant we may now be, we may reasonably aspire to a very high degree of glory and to the exquisite delights which come from a more intimate union with God. However insignificant we may be, and however low our position in this world, we may aspire to move in the highest society in Heaven.

And not only may we aspire to all this, and reach it, by the grace of God and the practice of virtue, but, what is more, we shall be made fit for our high position. For the moment the vision of God flashes upon our soul, we shall become like Him. We shall, therefore, be educated, filled with all knowledge, wisdom, and every other perfection. We shall be clothed with the personal beauty, refinement, and other graces which befit spouses of Jesus Christ and children of God. For you must ever bear in mind that the glory of Heaven, besides the elevation of our mind by the light of glory, implies the elevation of our whole nature to the supernatural state.

Therefore, not only is our mind elevated far beyond its present powers by the light of glory, but our body, also, is to be exalted by the resurrection far beyond its present perfection. As we have already seen, all the just are to rise in glory, but each one in his own degree of perfection. "For, one is the glory of the sun, another the glory of the moon, and another the glory of the stars. For star differeth from star in glory. So, also, in the resurrection of the dead."[87] Here the apostle of the Gentiles teaches us, in the plainest manner possible, that among the saints there is a very great difference in the degrees of personal beauty, grace, and splendor. There is as much difference between the beauty and splendor of the highest and those of the lowest, as we now see between the dazzling splendor of the sun and the pale light of the moon. As the resurrection is a portion of Heaven's rewards, it follows that the more completely we have mortified our inordinate passions and made our life conformable to that of Jesus Christ, the more personal beauty and splendor we shall possess in Heaven and, consequently, the more of Heaven's happiness we shall enjoy.

∞

Your heavenly beauty and perfection will reflect your holiness

These attributes of personal beauty and perfection and elevation to a high position in Heaven, are the very marks by which we shall immediately recognize those who have been most holy and who have done most for God in this world. It will no longer be as now, when the wicked prosper, possess wealth, honor, and power, while the virtuous are not unfrequently poor, despised, and even persecuted unto death.

Hence, the appearance of a man and his surroundings are not a rule by which we can rightly judge of his sanctity. Thus, when you see a man of great personal beauty, highly educated, and polished in his manners, surrounded with all the magnificence which the world can give, honored and idolized by his

[87] 1 Cor. 15:41-42.

fellows, enjoying a high social position, and all the pleasures of life, you do not — you cannot — judge, from all this worldly glory, that he is one of the holiest men living. He may, indeed, be a good man, but the glory which surrounds him is not the standard by which you can judge of the amount of virtue which he possesses.

In Heaven, the glory which surrounds the saints is a rule, and an infallible one, by which we can tell the amount of virtue they practiced while living in mortal flesh. Thus, when you enter there, you will see some who outshine others in splendor as the sun outshines the moon. You will see them wonderfully transformed into God, shining like the Divinity in His presence, partaking of the divine nature in a high degree, and united to Him in the most intimate manner. You will see them elevated far above others in rank, honored and loved in a special manner by the angels and saints. On seeing them, your first thought will be that these are the holiest persons in Heaven.

You will judge that their dazzling splendor, their wonderful resemblance to God, their intimate union with Him, the high position they occupy, and the exquisite pleasures they enjoy are all so many proofs that, while on earth, they loved God with their whole heart, and their neighbor as themselves, that they were poor in spirit, humble, pure, patient in adversity, and that perhaps some of them laid down their lives for God amid the most excruciating torments.

Here is a correct judgment. For it is precisely their heroic virtue, and not the mere accident of birth or the smile of fortune, which gives them the superior beauty, glory, and happiness they now enjoy.

∞

There are degrees of enjoyment
through the glorified senses

The possession and enjoyment of God in the Beatific Vision is not the whole happiness of man in Heaven, nor is it the only one in which there are different degrees of enjoyment. Our senses, as well as our minds, are to be elevated far beyond their present capacities for enjoyment. They, too, are to receive a supernatural development, an exquisite delicacy of perception, and the power of conveying pleasures to the soul, in proportion to the merits we have acquired by the holiness of our lives. Consequently, not only are those who have led the holiest lives the most intimately united to God, the most completely transformed into Him by partaking more abundantly of the divine nature, but their senses, also, are glorified and elevated in power of enjoyment far above the senses of those who have practiced virtue in an inferior degree. Hence, the highest in Heaven will receive immensely more pleasure through their senses than others whose lives have not been holy. Any contrary doctrine would savor of heresy.

If you were told, for instance, that a musician who never served God, but who, nevertheless, received the grace of a deathbed repentance, shall, on account of his cultivated musical ear, enjoy more pleasure from heavenly music than the Blessed Virgin and the holy virgins, your whole soul would undoubtedly revolt at such a doctrine. You would maintain that if Heaven is the reward of supernatural virtue, its whole happiness, its every joy, and its every delight, whether from God Himself or from creatures, should be enjoyed in a higher degree by those who have loved and served Him in a more perfect manner, and sacrificed themselves more completely for Him.

You would certainly be right in maintaining all this, for it is certainly so. The highest in Heaven will not only possess a greater elevation of mind — which is necessary to enjoy greater pleasure even from creatures — but their senses also will be more refined and acute and will, therefore, enable them to enjoy more refined pleasures from the objects of sense. It will be as already explained for the Beatific Vision. All shall see, hear, and otherwise enjoy the creatures prepared by the Almighty to rejoice the senses of His children; but all shall not, on that account, enjoy the same amount of pleasure. Each one shall receive his own pleasure, according to the supernatural perfection of his senses which he has deserved by the holiness of his life.

Let us endeavor to understand this by supposing a grand concert given in a church, where all classes of society are represented. All hear the music, both vocal and instrumental, and all, no doubt, receive pleasure. But do they all receive the same amount of pleasure? They certainly do not.

We may, for the sake of illustration, divide that vast assembly into three general classes. The first consists of those who have little or no musical ear, and, therefore, the concert affords them only an inferior pleasure. The next class is composed of those who have a good natural ear for music, but who never have developed and cultivated it by study. These evidently receive a far greater pleasure than the former. But the third class is composed of those who not only possess a natural talent for music, but who have, moreover, developed it by patient and assiduous study. These last receive unbounded pleasure. They follow with ease each instrument and voice into the most intricate harmony. They receive the most exquisite pleasure precisely in those parts where the uneducated perceive little or no beauty, because the music is too scientific for them.

Here you have the same object of pleasure for all. Everyone present hears the whole concert as if he were there alone — and yet, what a difference in the pleasure enjoyed by each one! We have divided these persons into three classes, but, in reality, each one forms a class by himself, for there are not two of those present, whether among the educated or the ignorant, who receive precisely the same amount of pleasure. Each one appropriates and enjoys his own individual pleasure, according to the peculiar development of his faculties.

So it is in Heaven. All the blessed hear the magnificent harmony, but all do not, on that account, enjoy the same degree of pleasure. Each one enjoys in proportion to his individual development, which is given him as a portion of his reward. And, as the reward is given in proportion to the holiness of their lives, it follows that the holiest enjoy more pleasure than others from heavenly music.

Evidently, this holds true of the other senses, which also are elevated and refined according to each one's holiness of life. Hence, however talented and learned a man may now be in music, astronomy, philosophy, poetry, or any other natural science, and however keen and perfect may be his senses, he will not enjoy more pleasure in virtue of these more perfect natural gifts, unless they have been consecrated to the service of God.

This is a truth which you must never forget. For it is to be feared that there is a half-formed notion in the minds of respectable and highly educated persons, that their superior talents and education will enable them to enjoy more of Heaven's happiness than those who either have no great talents or are too poor to have them developed by study. There can be no greater error. If it were so, the poor, who have already suffered so much from their humble position, would seemingly have reason to complain on seeing the educated classes again above them in Heaven — and merely on account of their higher education and other natural advantages. Remember that God can and will elevate each one in the power of enjoyment, according to the holiness of his life and not according to the natural advantages he enjoys in this world.

∞

You can use natural gifts
to increase your heavenly happiness

But although it is perfectly true that natural talents, as such, are not rewarded, and therefore do not elevate their possessors to a higher glory or power of enjoyment, the case is quite different if these talents have been developed under the influence of grace, and consecrated to God by supernatural motives. In such a supposition, they will most certainly be rewarded with a higher degree of glory and an increased power of enjoyment. Hence, philosophers, theologians, and other learned men, who study for the glory of God; poets, who sing the praises of God and of His saints; musicians, who devote their talents to the composition of sacred music; the men and the women who consecrate their talents and lives to the education of youth — these shall undoubtedly have their talents rewarded with an increased power of enjoyment, because they have supernaturalized them by a pure intention and exercised them for the glory of God and the salvation of souls.

The rich man will certainly not be higher in Heaven on account of his wealth, but he may increase his glory by making a proper use of his wealth. He may relieve the necessities of the fatherless and the widow. He may build up houses for the education of the poor. He may increase the beauty and the majesty of God's temples. And thus he may change his wealth into a means of reaching a very high degree of glory in Heaven.

So it is with you: if you are wealthy, talented, and highly educated, although you will not be higher in Heaven on account of these natural advantages, you may vastly increase your glory by being charitable toward the poor, by teaching the ignorant, by writing or translating good books, by purchasing and circulating such pious books among the poor, and by otherwise using your social position for the advancement of religion and glorifying God with the natural advantages He has so liberally bestowed upon you.

∽

There is no envy in Heaven

But you may, perhaps, ask, "Will not these different degrees of glory cause envy and, therefore, unhappiness in the lowest among the blessed? Will not kings and queens, and other great ones of this world be unhappy if they see the poor above them — when they see those, to whom they imagined they could not even speak without lowering their dignity, shining far above them in splendor?" I answer that if kings, queens, and other great ones of this world have the unspeakable good fortune of being admitted into Heaven, they certainly will not be envious of the greater glory they shall behold in those upon whom they formerly looked down.

There is no envy in Heaven. If we admit the possibility of such a thing as envy, then farewell to the happiness of Heaven. For in such a case no one could be happy. The lowest would envy the happiness of those who are a little higher, and these would envy the happiness of the highest. And these would envy the happiness of the Blessed Virgin, and she, too, would be unhappy, because she does not possess the glory of the Hypostatic Union, which is the privilege of Jesus Christ alone. The absurdity of all this is a sufficient answer to the question.

Each one in Heaven is satisfied with his own lot, because it suits him and no one else. As St. Augustine says: When a tall man and a little boy are both dressed in a suit of the same precious cloth, each is suited and fitted to his satisfaction. The little boy is neither envious nor unhappy because the tall man has more cloth than he; and he certainly would not exchange with him. So it is also in Heaven. Everyone there is satisfied with his own degree of glory, because it suits him and gratifies all the rational cravings of his nature. Not only are the lowest without envy, and perfectly satisfied with their degree of glory, but they even rejoice at the higher glory of others. For they see that those who enjoy the highest glory of Heaven have deserved it by the heroic virtues they practiced while on earth.

Christian soul, I suppose that now you understand something of the degrees of enjoyment in Heaven, and that you are filled with noble ambition to reach a high degree of union with God. You no doubt desire to see your whole nature so elevated as to have the most perfect enjoyment of God Himself and of the creatures in store to rejoice the glorified senses of the just.

Set to work in good earnest to live a holy life, for it is by so doing that we deserve the highest powers of enjoyment. A few days of labor and struggle, a few days of self-denial, a few days of suffering, and then comes the undisturbed possession and enjoyment of God Himself and of His beautiful and pure creatures, forever! This is what is in store for those who practice virtue and persevere unto the end.

Chapter Fifteen

∞

You will see the special glory of the blessed

Before entering upon contemplation of the excellent glory which surrounds the blessed in Heaven, we must endeavor to form a correct idea of God's grace, which enabled the blessed to perform the great and noble actions we are now to consider. They were all, except Jesus and Mary, conceived in sin, and, therefore, subject to the same temptations that daily assail us. They never could have triumphed and reached the supernatural glory which now surrounds them, had they been left to their own natural strength, or rather, weakness.

When we enter a well-cultivated garden, filled with flowers of every color and every degree of beauty, it never enters into our minds that they grew so of themselves, or gave to themselves their delicate and exquisite perfumes. We know that the gardener's skill had something to do with their growth and beauty. We know, too, that rain and sunshine, the soil's quality, and other natural influences did what was totally beyond the gardener's power. Finally, we come to God, who is ultimately the sole Author of their very life, growth, and perfection.

We are now to enter God's glorious garden to contemplate the beauty of the flowers which He has planted and beautified by His grace. Every saint is like a flower, beautiful in proportion to the amount of grace he received, and also in proportion to the degree of his own free cooperation with this grace. Some received the grace of the apostleship; others received the grace of martyrdom; others received the grace of the priesthood; others the grace of trampling underfoot the honors and pleasures of this world by consecrating themselves to God in religious communities; while others, again, received the grace of becoming saints while living in the world. Thus each one, by corresponding with his own grace, which gave him a supernatural strength, reached the glory to which he is entitled.

No one in the whole of Heaven can say that he enjoys its happiness by his own natural endeavors, for, without the grace of God, we cannot even have a good thought, or pronounce the name of Jesus, so as to deserve a supernatural reward. Hence, the highest in Heaven must say, with St. Paul, "By the grace of God I am what I am. And His grace in me hath not been void, but I have labored more abundantly than all they; yet not I, but the grace of God with me."[88]

It is by the aid of this grace that the blessed have reached the glory of Heaven; it is by this all-powerful grace that they have deserved the unfading crown, of which St. Paul speaks so boldly and confidently, when he says, "I have fought a good fight; I have finished my course; I have kept the faith. As to the rest, there is laid up for me a crown of justice, which the Lord, the just Judge, will render to me at that day; and not to me only, but to them also who love His coming."[89] This is the

---

[88] 1 Cor. 15:10.
[89] 2 Tim. 4:7-8.

glorious crown we are now to consider — and first of all, in Jesus Christ, who, in His human nature, is elevated and glorified far above all in Heaven.

Jesus is the Son of God, but He is also "the Son of Man."[90] As God, His glory is from everlasting to everlasting. It had no beginning, and it shall have no end. As its source is in His very essence, it can be neither increased nor diminished. But it is far different with the glory of the human nature which He assumed. That had a beginning, and could be increased, and, as a matter of fact, was increased, until He exalted it above all that is not God, in Heaven. Let us now contemplate His bright glory and rejoice with Him in His surpassing blessedness.

∽

Jesus' happiness surpasses that of the blessed

See Jesus enthroned at the right hand of God His Father, clothed with "great power and majesty."[91] The personal union of the eternal Son of God with the human nature gives Him, as man, undisputed pre-eminence over all, in power, holiness, beauty, and every other attribute communicable to a created nature. He is so completely possessed, embraced, and penetrated by the divine nature that His adorable Heart is the throne of the most perfect happiness ever enjoyed by man. That loving Heart, which is purer than the sun's brightest rays, is filled to overflowing with the most exquisite joys emanating from the very heart of the most Holy Trinity.

[90] Matt. 9:6.
[91] Cf. Matt. 24:30.

The Happiness of Heaven

While on earth, no one ever loved God and man as Jesus did; and now there is none in all the heavens who is equally loved in return, both by God Himself and the bright throngs that surround His throne. No man, therefore, ever did or ever can enjoy a happiness so pure, so exquisite, and in so eminent a degree as He does.

While on earth, His soul was "sorrowful even unto death,"[92] but now it is inebriated with torrents of joy, too great for poor human language to express. While on earth, He likewise suffered in all His senses. He endured hunger and thirst, cold and heat, fatigue, and the numberless privations which His poverty entailed upon Him. But it was especially during His cruel Passion that His sight, hearing, taste, and particularly His sense of feeling, were tortured to the utmost; and now His glorified senses have become the avenues of the most exquisite and refined pleasures.

He now sees Himself surrounded by the thousands whom His Precious Blood has sanctified and beautified, and He continually hears the sweet harmony of their grateful songs. His sacred body, which had been bruised and mangled, disfigured and dishonored by the filthy spittle of His enemies, is now the most beautiful, perfect, and resplendent in the whole kingdom of Heaven. It is the very sun which, by its splendor, gives beauty and life to the whole of Heaven.[93] In a word, Jesus, as man, is above all in power, majesty, wisdom, and glory, and He enjoys the most perfect and complete happiness that ever came from God.

[92] Matt. 26:38.
[93] Cf. Rev. 21:23.

∞

Jesus enjoys the highest glory because of His merits

But you will, perhaps, say, "Does not Jesus enjoy all this un-speakable glory, simply and exclusively in virtue of His high privileges? Is it not on account of the Hypostatic Union that He is thus exalted above all in glory?" I answer: Although the Hypostatic Union, by its very nature, gives Him the right to the first place in Heaven, it gives Him neither the glory nor the rewards which are due to Him as the Redeemer of mankind. The Hypostatic Union is a high privilege, a free gift of God, which Jesus did not merit, for that privilege, in the designs of His Father, involved the office of Redeemer. This was His vocation in this world, and He corresponded to it faithfully. He taught the world, first by example, next by His heavenly doctrines. Then He submitted willingly, and even cheerfully, to all the indignities of His bitter Passion, and finally consummated the great work of man's redemption by expiring upon the Cross.

It is for all this life of poverty, suffering, and humiliation that He is rewarded and so wonderfully glorified, and not exclusively on account of the Hypostatic Union. Listen to St. Paul, and he will tell you why Jesus is exalted above all in Heaven: "He humbled Himself, becoming obedient unto death, even the death of the Cross. For which cause God hath also exalted Him, and hath given Him a name which is above all names, that at the name of Jesus, every knee should bow of those that are in Heaven, on earth, and under the earth."[94] Surely this is far from saying that Jesus enjoys the highest glory of Heaven

---

[94] Phil. 2:8-10.

exclusively on account of the Hypostatic Union. It is given to Him by His Father as a "crown of justice," which He really deserved by His sufferings and obedience unto the death of the Cross.

It is, moreover, the beautiful canticle which forever resounds through the vaults of Heaven. Listen to it: "Thou art worthy, O Lord, to take the book and open the seals thereof; because Thou wast slain and hast redeemed us in Thy blood, out of every tribe, and tongue, and people, and nation."[95] It is evident, then, that Jesus is rewarded in His human nature with the highest glory of Heaven on account of His own individual merits.

∞

Mary's glory is second only to Jesus'

Let us now spend a few moments in contemplating the glory of the Blessed Virgin. Jesus is the King of Heaven; Mary is the Queen. She certainly comes next to Jesus in dignity and merit, and her glory is, therefore, next to His in splendor and magnificence. She is the woman of whom the beloved disciple speaks when he says, "And a great wonder appeared in Heaven: a woman clothed with the sun, and the moon under her feet, and on her head a crown of twelve stars."[96] This certainly expresses the highest glory and splendor imaginable. Human words can say nothing more, for our highest ideas of glory are borrowed from those beautiful worlds that shine above us in the blue ether.

[95] Rev. 5:9.
[96] Rev. 12:1.

On her bosom she wears a jewel of unsurpassed splendor, whereon are written her three singular privileges: Immaculate, Mother of God and Virgin. These are high privileges which she alone enjoys and which single her out at once as the Queen of angels and of men.

The Eternal, by assuming flesh from her, united her to Himself by a bond of intimacy which is second only to that of the Hypostatic Union. The almighty Father shed His own bright glory around Mary and enthroned her at the right hand of Jesus. He looks upon her with complacency, as His own beloved daughter, faultless in beauty and every other perfection.

The Holy Spirit calls her His own spotless and faithful spouse, over whom the breath of sin never passed, while Jesus who, in all His glory, is still flesh of her flesh, and bone of her bone, calls her His own sweet and loving mother. Can we conceive any greater glory — unless it be that of the Hypostatic Union?

In this world, a great king may see with grief that many other women surpass his own mother, daughter, or spouse in beauty, intelligence, virtue, and other perfections; but, however grieved he may be, he is totally powerless to remedy this evil, and he must continue to see others outshining those who are dearest to his heart. This is not so in Heaven. Never shall it be said in Heaven that there are women holier, purer, more intelligent, or more beautiful than the Blessed Virgin. For God has the power to clothe her with attributes that will forever make her superior to any mere creature. Not only does He have the power, but as a matter of fact, *He has* adorned her by bestowing upon her every gift of nature, grace, and glory, in an eminent degree. She, above all saints, is "full of grace,"[97] and is made a partaker of the divine nature, and, therefore, her Immaculate Heart, which is purer than crystal, is the home of the most perfect happiness ever enjoyed by woman.

∞

Mary enjoys high glory because of her merit
But, remember well, Mary does not enjoy all this excellent glory exclusively on account of her glorious privileges. These are, like those of Jesus, free gifts of God, which she did not merit. But she freely and generously corresponded to all the designs of God, and, therefore, she is rewarded with the highest glory of Heaven. She, too, as well as Jesus, was obedient unto death. She, too, was submissive to the most trying dispensations of Providence. She, too, suffered patiently from every manner of privation, for she was poor. She, too, endured the most bitter anguish during the Passion of her beloved Son, and had her pure soul overwhelmed with agonies of which we can form no adequate conception. Hence, God hath also exalted her and given her a name which is above every name except that of Jesus.

Thus we see that even Jesus and Mary, the bright King and Queen of Heaven, are exalted above all angels and men in glory, on account of the heroic virtue they both practiced in this world, and not exclusively in virtue of their dignity and high privileges. They both labored for it, both suffered for it, and both deserved it as a "crown of justice," which a just Judge bestowed upon them as a reward of merit.

[97] Luke 1:28.

∞

St. Joseph enjoys a high degree of glory

It is impossible to think of Jesus and Mary without, at the same time, thinking of the illustrious St. Joseph. He is so intimately bound up with them that we can neither forget him nor separate him from them.

He was emphatically a hidden saint. He was truly "a just man,"[98] as the Holy Spirit calls him. He was so humble, so pure, so unspeakably charitable to the Blessed Virgin. Then, too, he loved Jesus so much, so tenderly, and took such great care of Him during His infancy. Whenever he received a command, he always obeyed so promptly, without excuse or murmur, although at times the commands involved great privations and sufferings.

In a word, St. Joseph, too, corresponded with the grace of his sublime vocation, and he now shines with exceeding glory near Jesus and Mary. He, too, is glorified on account of his tender love for God, for Jesus and Mary, and for his neighbor, and not exclusively in virtue of the glorious privilege of having been the guardian of Mary's purity and the foster-father of Jesus. Therefore, his exceeding glory is also a "crown of justice," with which a just Judge has encircled his brow.

∞

The martyrs show the greatest love

We shall now contemplate the glory of the vast multitude of the Blessed, who surround the thrones of Jesus and Mary. I quote from the book of Revelation: "After this, I saw a great

---

[98] Matt. 1:19.

multitude, which no man could number, of all nations, and tribes, and peoples, and tongues, standing before the throne, and in the sight of the Lamb, clothed with white robes and palms in their hands."[99] This glorious multitude represents all the blessed. They may be divided into eight classes: the martyrs, the doctors and confessors, the virgins, the religious, the penitents, the pious people, those of inferior virtue, and the baptized infants. In this chapter we shall consider the glory of the martyrs.

See that beautiful army of martyrs — those brave soldiers of Jesus Christ — who died for Him and, like Him, in the midst of the most cruel torments. Theirs is truly a "crown of justice." They are represented as holding palms in their hands, in token of the victory which they gained over the world. Their intimate union with God, the dazzling splendor of their personal appearance, and the high honors conferred upon them single them out at once as those champions of the Faith who, while on earth, served God in a heroic degree.

And they certainly served Him with distinction, for they proved their love by laying down their lives for Him. Laying down one's life for God has always been looked upon as the most perfect act of love possible, for "greater love than this no man hath: that a man lay down his life for his friends."[100] Hence, the martyrs, as a class, have always been considered as deserving the highest honors of Heaven.

The beautiful words of the Holy Spirit in reference to all the just apply with peculiar force to the martyrs: "But the souls

[99] Rev. 7:9.
[100] John 15:13.

of the just are in the hand of God, and the torment of death shall not touch them. In the sight of the unwise they seemed to die, and their departure was taken for misery, and their going away from us, for utter destruction; but they are in peace. And although in the sight of men they suffered torments, their hope is full of immortality. Afflicted in a few things, in many they shall be rewarded, because God hath tried them, and found them worthy of Himself. As gold in the furnace He hath proved them; and as the victim of a holocaust He hath received them."[101]

What a bright and beautiful crowd they are! As a garden is beautified by flowers, so is Heaven made more beautiful by the radiant, crimson-clad army of martyrs. Here is St. John the Baptist, the fearless precursor of Jesus. Here is the glorious St. Stephen, the first who laid down his life after the Ascension of Jesus. Here are the holy Apostles, those intrepid soldiers of Christ, who went forth from the council, rejoicing that they had been found worthy to suffer for the name of Jesus.[102] The prediction of their divine Master was verified in them: "For they shall deliver you up in councils, and they will scourge you in their synagogues. And you shall be brought before governors, and before kings for my sake. . . . And you shall be hated by all men for my sake."[103] "Yea, the hour cometh that whosoever killeth you, will think that he doeth a service to God."[104]

---

[101]Wisd. 3:1-6.
[102]Acts 5:41.
[103]Matt. 10:17-18, 22.
[104]John 16:2.

The Happiness of Heaven

∞

The martyrs trusted in Christ's promises

But in spite of all this hatred and persecution, they sowed the seed of the word of God in the hearts of men and watered it with their own blood. They now enjoy a special glory in Heaven, for, besides the glory which belongs to them as martyrs, they also enjoy that which belongs to them as Apostles, promised to them in these words of our blessed Lord: "Amen, I say to you, that you, who have followed me, in the regeneration, when the Son of Man shall sit on the seat of His majesty, you shall also sit on twelve seats, judging the twelve tribes of Israel."[105]

Here are also so many holy popes and bishops and priests, the worthy successors of the Apostles, who, like them, joyfully laid down their lives for the love of Jesus Christ. Here is also that countless multitude of holy missionaries who, like the Apostles, went forth into all nations to preach the gospel. They, too, were "brought before governors, and before kings," and sealed their Faith with their blood. Here, too, are holy virgins who preferred death, in all its horrid shapes, rather than stain their souls or have another spouse besides Jesus, to whom they had consecrated themselves. The grace of God changed them from timid, retiring virgins, into dauntless heroines and enabled them to suffer death with superhuman courage and constancy.

Here are also married men and women, fathers and mothers who loved God more than they loved their children. Here, even, are little children, who astounded the heartless tyrants

---

[105]Matt. 19:28.

by the admirable patience and heroism which they displayed amid the most refined cruelties. Here, too, are venerable old men and women who, in spite of the infirmities of age, ascended the scaffold with a firm step and suffered death with undaunted constancy.

All these, like St. Paul, have fought a good fight, and all, without exception, have received a "crown of justice" at the hands of a just Judge. They all enjoy the high rewards which Jesus promised to His heroic followers when He said, "Blessed are they that suffer persecution for justice's sake: for theirs is the kingdom of Heaven. Blessed are you when men shall revile you, and persecute you, and shall say all manner of evil against you falsely, for my sake: rejoice, and be exceeding glad: because your reward is very great in Heaven."[106]

∞

The martyrs enjoy different degrees of glory

But, before leaving these to consider the glory of others, we must remark that, although they are all martyrs, they do not, on that account, all enjoy the same degree of glory. They are all stars, but "star differeth from star in glory."[107] Each martyr is clothed in his own brightness, which is great in proportion to the intensity of his love for God and the amount of suffering endured for Him. Some were simply put to death, without any additional torture. Others were imprisoned, scourged, and then put to death. Still others again were tortured for days, weeks, and even months, with the most frightful torments.

[106]Cf. Matt. 5:10-12.
[107]1 Cor. 15:41.

Again, some came to their martyrdom totally devoid of any previous virtue — some even loaded with sin, and unbaptized — but they received a baptism of blood, which made them pure and deserved for them the high honors of Heaven. Nevertheless, the glory that surrounds such is far inferior to that which surrounds those who, like St. John the Baptist, St. Peter, St. Paul, St. Andrew, and a host of others, came to their martyrdom loaded with the merits of a life spent in the practice of heroic virtue.

∞

All who spread the Faith
enjoy a special glory

Let us now turn our eyes to another bright throng. It is composed of the doctors and confessors of the Church. These, too, as well as the martyrs, enjoy the high honors of Heaven. Here we meet again the Apostles, who were filled with the Holy Spirit and instructed the infant Church in all truth. There, too, are their worthy successors in the ministry — such men as St. John Chrysostom,[108] St. Augustine, St. Gregory,[109] St. Thomas, and a multitude of others — whose vast intellects were stored with the knowledge of God. They gained a signal victory over the Devil who is the "father of lies."[110] By their eloquence, and by their writings, they enlightened the Church, not only in their day, but for all time to come. They are now crowned with the particular glory which is promised to all

[108]St. John Chrysostom (c. 347-407), Bishop of Constantinople.
[109]Possibly St. Gregory I (c. 540-604), Pope from 590. — ED.
[110]John 8:44.

such: "They that are learned shall shine as the brightness of the firmament, and they that instruct many unto justice, as the stars for all eternity."[111]

But you must not imagine that the great lights of Christianity, such as the Apostles, St. Augustine, St. Thomas, and others, who have been proclaimed doctors of the Church, are alone in their glory. This class also includes the glorious confessors of the Church — all holy popes, bishops, and priests who have zealously and faithfully preached the gospel to their flocks. It comprises also all those holy missionaries who, like the Apostles, preached Jesus crucified to the heathens and brought them into the one true fold. These holy confessors, although not proclaimed doctors by the Church, nevertheless shine "as the stars for all eternity."

But, besides these glorious confessors, there are still others who partake of the special reward promised to those who "instruct many unto justice." These are the innumerable multitudes of men and women who compose the different religious orders of the Church who spend their lives in the education of youth. There are, moreover, the writers, translators, and publishers of good books, and others, who, although not bound by any vows, devote themselves to the diffusion of religious knowledge. Among these, particular mention must be made of good parents, whose first care is to teach the knowledge and love of God to their children.

In a word, all they who have, in any way, instructed others unto justice partake of the special glory of the doctors and confessors of the Church, although, no doubt, in an inferior

[111]Dan. 12:3.

degree. For the promise of a special reward is not made exclusively to a few gifted intellects, but to all, without any exception. "They that shall instruct many unto justice shall shine as the stars for all eternity."

∞

Preaching the Gospel must be accompanied by holiness

Yet, although it is true that instructing others unto justice deserves a special reward, we must not forget that the preaching of the gospel will not, of itself, glorify anyone unless it is accompanied by a pure intention and the practice of virtue. This is what our blessed Lord tells us in the most positive manner when He says, "He that shall do and teach, He shall be called great in the kingdom of Heaven."[112] Hence, you must ever remember that, however gifted you may be, however eloquent, and however many you may have taught unto justice, you never can shine as a star in Heaven unless you lead a Christian life at the same time. Without this, your preaching will profit you nothing, even if others are saved by your eloquence.

∞

The holy virgins chose Christ as their spouse

There are two other bright throngs that present themselves. They are the holy virgins and the religious. Let us first contemplate the bright glory of the virgins. I quote again from the book of Revelation: "And I heard a great voice from Heaven. . . . And the voice which I heard was as the voice of

[112]Matt. 5:19.

harpers . . . harping upon their harps. And they sang, as it were, a new canticle before the throne. . . . And no man could say that canticle but those hundred and forty-four thousand. . . . These are they who were not defiled with women, for they are virgins. These follow the Lamb whithersoever He goeth."[113]

These evidently form a distinct class in Heaven. It is composed of both men and women who never married and never lost their virtue by actual sin. I speak here of such as these, and not of any others. Hence, we must exclude from this class all little children who died before they could be responsible for their deeds, for, although they all died virgins, their virginity, which was a gift of nature, does not deserve a "crown of justice." Therefore, in this place we shall consider the excellent glory only of those, who, having grown to the age of discretion, led a life of purity and died virgins. Evidently, these alone have purchased the glory promised to virgins.

Many of these virgins led holy lives while living in the world — either with or without vow — while the great majority were so enraptured with the beauty and purity of Jesus that they cheerfully gave up all the lawful pleasures of the world and consecrated themselves to Him by the vows of poverty, chastity, and obedience. In this life of suffering and self-denial, they persevered unto the end.

Their day of trial and suffering is now over, and they are rewarded with exceeding glory. Clad in their white robes, which denote the spotless purity of their lives, they enjoy a special intimate union with Jesus, their beloved Spouse. While on earth, they would have no other spouse but Him.

[113]Rev. 14:2-4.

The Happiness of Heaven

They consecrated themselves to Him, and He accepted the noble sacrifice. By His grace He sanctified and beautified them and made them worthy of the special glory they now enjoy. How beautiful they are! How glorious! They are the lilies of Heaven. In the words of the Holy Spirit, we may exclaim, "Oh, how beautiful is the chaste generation with glory, for the memory thereof is immortal, because it is known both with God and with men. When it is present, they imitate it, and they desire it when it hath withdrawn itself, and it triumpheth forever, winning the reward of undefiled conflicts."[114]

∞

Virginity must be accompanied by virtue

Yet, while it is true that those who die virgins are rewarded with a special glory, we must not forget that virginity alone can neither deserve the high honors of Heaven, nor even save anyone, unless it is accompanied by the virtues which befit a spouse of Christ. There are many foolish virgins who are not even admitted to the wedding feast, because they are not adorned with charity and other virtues which belong to their state.[115]

We must ever remember that the crown worn by the virgins in Heaven is only an accidental glory, for if it were essential, no one except virgins could be happy there. Virginity is, therefore, far from being the greatest of virtues, or the most necessary to reach the high honors of Heaven. For, to use the strong language of the apostle Paul, if you could speak with the

[114]Wisd. 4:1-2.
[115]Cf. Matt. 25:1-12.

tongues of angels and men; and if you knew all mysteries, and had all knowledge; and if you had faith, so as to move mountains, and have not charity — even though you be a virgin — you are become as sounding brass and a tinkling cymbal.[116] Neither will your virginity, nor all other gifts, profit you anything without charity.

See, therefore, that you endeavor to clothe your soul with those virtues which befit a spouse of Jesus Christ. Love God above all things. Be extremely charitable to all. Be humble, modest, and reserved. Lead a life of mortification, silence, and prayer. For unless you lead such a life as your vocation requires, you expose yourself to hear the terrible words spoken to the foolish virgins. When they came to the wedding, they stood at the door and said, " 'Lord, Lord, open to us.' But He answering, said, 'Amen, I say to you, I know you not.' "[117]

But if you do lead the charitable life of a true spouse of Christ, you shall undoubtedly reach a high degree of glory in Heaven. You will wear the virgins' crown and enjoy the special intimate union with Jesus which is promised to all those who, despising the short-lived pleasures of this world, have consecrated themselves to His divine service.

∽

Religious give up all for Christ

Let us now spend a few moments in contemplating the high glory of the religious. This class is composed exclusively of men and women who, while on earth, consecrated themselves

---

[116]Cf. 1 Cor. 13:1-2.
[117]Matt. 25:11-12.

to God by the vows of poverty, chastity, and obedience. Many of them — perhaps the great majority — are virgins, while others are not. For many of them, like St. Francis Borgia,[118] were widowers; and others, like St. Frances of Rome,[119] were widows. There are others who, when young and foolish, committed sin by which they may have ceased to be virgins, but who nevertheless received a most marked vocation to the religious life. All these, as well as virgins, enjoy a special glory in Heaven, which is due to them as a "crown of justice" on account of the great sacrifices they made to God by the vows of religion.

By the vow of poverty, they not only stripped themselves of all their possessions, but also gave up the natural right which all men have to possess property. By the vow of chastity, they gave up the natural right which all men have to enjoy the lawful pleasures of the body. By the vow of obedience, they not only relinquished forever the right to dispose of themselves, but they also placed themselves in the hands of their superiors, to be ruled and governed by them as if they were mere children. Thus, by one single act, religious persons abandon all that is dearest to the heart of man according to nature, for they not only give up all their possessions — the world, with its honors and pleasures — they not only sacrifice their liberty, but they also abandon father and mother, brother and sister, friends and relatives. In a word, they cut themselves off from the world and all that makes life bright and desirable, according to

---

[118]St. Francis Borgia (1510-1572), Jesuit priest.

[119]St. Frances of Rome (1384-1440), foundress of the Oblates of St. Benedict of Tor de' Specchi.

nature. And what is more, they embrace a life of continual mortification and self-denial.

It is true that the grace of God, which enables men and women to make such sacrifices, makes the life of the religious tolerable; but this does not prevent it from being a life of a continual and painful struggle against the inclinations and cravings of nature. From all this, it follows that religious, as such, whether virgins or not, enjoy an exceeding glory in Heaven on account of the sublime sacrifice of themselves they have made to God by the three vows of religion. This is what our blessed Lord promises when He says, "And every one that hath left house, or brethren, or sisters, or father, or mother, or wife, or children, or lands for my name's sake shall receive a hundredfold, and shall possess life everlasting."[120]

In speaking of the three vows, theologians compare them to martyrdom. They maintain that, as a man who lays down his life for the Faith enters Heaven immediately, without any detention in Purgatory, so also does a religious who dies immediately after taking his vows. Whatever temporal punishment was due to him on account of his sins is entirely canceled by that one act. And the reason they give is that the act of sacrificing oneself to God by the vows of religion is, like martyrdom, one of the noblest and most heroic acts that man can perform.

If, then, virgins, as such, are rewarded with a special glory in Heaven, what shall we say of the glory and splendor which surrounds religious? For virgins make only one great sacrifice, by the practice of perfect chastity, while religious, who make

[120]Matt. 19:29.

the same sacrifice, add to this two others: poverty and obedience. And experience teaches that these two additional vows are, for most persons, far more difficult, because they involve far more suffering and self-denial than the mere practice of chastity. From all this, it follows that virgins who are of a religious order, enjoy a far higher degree of glory in Heaven than those who are not religious. It follows, also, that religious, as such, whether virgins or not, enjoy an exceeding glory in Heaven, in virtue of the great sacrifices they have made for God by the three vows of religion. Like Jesus, they were poor, chaste, and obedient unto death; and like Him also, they are exalted to the high honors of Heaven.

∞

Religious enjoy different degrees of glory

But, although it is true that religious, as such, enjoy a high degree of glory in Heaven, it must not be inferred that they all enjoy the same degree of glory. There is, perhaps, not a class in Heaven in which the degrees of glory are so various. Some of them died only a few days after taking their vows; others, on the day itself; while others lived half a century or more in the practice of the most heroic virtue. Some were called by the grace of God after a life of worldliness and sin; while others had already reached a high degree of sanctity when they offered their sacrifice to God. Others again, after their consecration to God, were extremely faithful to grace and gave all the energies of their nature to the acquirement of greater perfection; while others were sadly wanting in generosity to God and aimed at only an inferior degree of holiness. Again, some had few or no temptations from the day upon which they took their vows; while, for others, that act seemed to be a declaration of war, for they began to be assailed by every manner of temptation to violate their vows and go back into the world. But, aided by the all-powerful grace of God, they resisted manfully and fought the good fight unto the end.

These, and a thousand other differences, give rise to various degrees of glory among the religious, who, having finished their course, have received the crown of life. Those who, like St. Aloysius, St. Stanislaus, St. Teresa,[121] and many others, practiced every virtue in a heroic degree, are among the brightest and the highest in glory, while they who led less perfect lives are far inferior. Nevertheless, all, without exception, enjoy a special glory which is due to them as a "crown of justice" for the great sacrifice they made to God by the three vows of religion.

∞

Penitents and pious people enjoy special glory
Who are they that compose the bright multitude of penitents and pious people? They are headed by a queen who does not wear a virgin's crown; and yet, she is so beautiful and enjoys so intimate a union with Jesus. Who is she? She is Mary Magdalene, the bright queen of penitents and the star of hope to all who have grievously sinned in this world.

She was once a sinner — and such a sinner! Her soul was the home of seven devils! She was a hireling of Satan to catch

---

[121]St. Aloysius Gonzaga (1568-1591), Jesuit and patron saint of youth; St. Stanislaus Kostka (1550-1568), Jesuit novice; St. Teresa of Lisieux (1873-1897), Carmelite nun.

the souls of men. But a flash of light came forth from the Heart of Jesus, and in that light she saw herself sinful and hateful in the eyes of God. His grace filled her heart with a deep and crushing sorrow for her many sins. Prostrate at the feet of Jesus, she kissed them and washed them with the tears of true repentance. Her many sins were forgiven her, because she loved much;[122] for her deep contrition was not dictated by servile fear, but by pure love. Her intense love and her penitential tears deserved for her a "crown of justice." They beautified and glorified her far above many who never sinned grievously, for she is crowned with the high honors of Heaven and enjoys a union with Jesus far more intimate than many who never offended God.

And she is not alone in this exceeding glory with which sinners are clothed through ardent love and penance. Thousands of others who sinned grievously and imitated Mary Magdalene's penance are now shining in glory far above others who never sinned. Do you think that St. Peter, who denied his Lord, is below *all* those who preserved their innocence, and even below all the baptized infants in Heaven? Do you think that St. Paul, who once persecuted the Church, is now below *all* on that account? Do you think that the great St. Augustine, St. Mary of Egypt, St. Pelagia, and a host of other illustrious penitents, are all below mere babies on account of their sins? They certainly are not. Their intense love for God, their sorrow, and their tears atoned for their sins, and placed them far, very far, above many who, although they never sinned grievously, never performed an act of heroic virtue in their whole lives.

[122]Luke 7:37-38, 47.

Remember that charity — by which is meant love for God
and for our neighbor — is the greatest of virtues and has the
power of elevating the greatest sinners to the highest glory of
Heaven. Mary Magdalene, therefore, although once a great
sinner, is, at this moment enjoying an intimate union with Jesus, and she shines like a very star in the presence of God.

Even in this world she is glorified far above many who
were not sinners. When Jesus sat at the table of Simon the
leper, Mary Magdalene anointed Him with precious oint-
ment. Some of the Apostles complained of the waste, but Jesus
defended her conduct and added, "Amen, I say to you, where-
soever this gospel shall be preached, that also which she hath
done, shall be told for a memorial of her."[123] Again, we read in
the Gospel of St. Mark, that Jesus, "rising early the first day of
the week, appeared first to Mary Magdalene, from whom He
had cast out seven devils."[124] Again, in the Litany of the
Saints, the Church places the name of Mary Magdalene before
all the virgins. This is certainly a high honor. There is, moreover, a congregation of Magdalenes, of which she is the model
and patroness. It is attached to the order of the Good Shep-
herd, and is filled, not only with women who have sinned, but
with virgins, too, who have fallen in love with the beautiful
penitential spirit of Mary Magdalene.

All this must certainly be very consoling to those who
have sinned grievously, and who have, perhaps, thought that,
on account of their sins, they have lost all right to a high place
in Heaven. Mary Magdalene, St. Peter, St. Augustine, and a

[123]Matt. 26:13.
[124]Mark 16:9.

The Happiness of Heaven

host of other illustrious penitents, teach us that a high degree
of glory is ours — no matter what sins we have committed —
if we love ardently, lead a penitential life, and practice other
virtues in an eminent degree.

∞

Holy people from all walks of life are in Heaven

There is one more beautiful throng standing around the
throne of God and enjoying a high degree of glory in Heaven.
It is made up of the vast multitude of men and women who
sanctified themselves while living in the world. They are
known as the pious. They lived in the world, but were not of it.
They did not live according to its spirit, for its spirit is the
sworn enemy of God. Many of them, while surrounded with
the wealth and magnificence of this world, practiced the virtues of the cloister. Others belonged to the middle classes of
society, and others, again, to the poorer classes. But in whatever class their lot was cast, they all sanctified themselves by
loving God and their neighbor, and by acquitting themselves
of their respective duties. What a beautiful and glorious throng
they are!

Here are kings and queens who, in their exalted position,
knew how to be humble and who used their wealth and position for the benefit of their subjects. Here are representatives
of all professions and trades in society — lawyers, physicians,
soldiers, tradesmen, and cultivators of the soil. Here, too, are
the servants of the rich who thought it a kindness to be allowed to do all drudgery in order to have wherewithal to live.
Here are good husbands and wives who truly loved each other
and were faithful unto death. Here are those good parents

whose first care was to teach their children the knowledge and love of God. Here, too, are the good children who honored their parents and cared for them with a tender charity when age and infirmity had rendered them helpless. Here, too, are young men and young women who, although they had no call to consecrate their virginity to Jesus Christ, led the lives of angels amid the fascinations of the world.

All these have led pious lives. They mortified their passions. They were given to prayer. They frequented the sacraments. They performed acts of charity according to their means and practiced the virtues of their rank and calling.

All these have therefore reached the honors and distinctions which God distributes among those who have served Him with fidelity. Although they are neither martyrs nor doctors nor religious, they all led holy lives; they all have received a "crown of justice," which was due to them as a reward for their love of God and for the virtues they practiced while on earth. Many of them were great saints, such as St. Louis, king of France; St. Elizabeth, queen of Portugal; St. Monica, widow; St. Genevieve, the virgin shepherdess; St. Zita, the angelic servant-girl; and many others, whom the Church has placed upon her altars, and proposed to our imitation.

∞

All are called to a high degree of glory

You see, then, that the high honors of Heaven do not belong, exclusively, to any privileged classes, as you might imagine the martyrs, doctors, virgins, and religious to be. A high degree of glory is offered to all and, by the grace of God, is attainable by all, without any exception. If, therefore, you have until now looked upon it as a presumption to aim at a high degree of glory, because you were neither a consecrated virgin nor a religious, banish such a thought from your mind. For, instead of being a presumption, it is a virtue to aspire to a high sanctity and, consequently, to a high degree of union with God in Heaven.

Therefore, whether you are married or single, rich or poor, learned or ignorant, you are called upon by your Lord Jesus to fight the good fight unto the end, with a solemn assurance that, when you have finished your course, a just Judge will encircle your brow with a "crown of justice" and admit you into the society of those who signalized themselves in His service.

∞

God's mercy and liberality admit others into Heaven

Before closing this chapter, we must say a few words, at least, about the two remaining classes of the blessed — probably, by far the most numerous in Heaven. One is composed of those who were not pious or generous to God. Many of them sinned often, and grievously, and did very little to atone for their sins. The virtues they practiced were few and never brought to any perfection. This class also includes all those who spent their whole lives in sin and who were saved, like the thief on the cross,[125] by the grace of a deathbed repentance. Evidently, neither these nor others who practiced scarcely any virtue are crowned with the high honors of Heaven, which are the reward of a virtuous life. They are, nevertheless, perfectly happy, in their own degree, and sing the mercies of God, who

[125]Cf. Luke 23:39-43.

saved many of them almost in spite of themselves. Theirs may be called a crown of mercy, rather than one of justice.

The other class is composed of baptized infants and of children who died before they were responsible for their deeds. But in Heaven they are no longer children, for their elevation to glory has developed them into men and women. They therefore enjoy the full perfection of human nature, as well as those who died adults.[126] They are, moreover, admitted to the Beatific Vision, and, consequently, they see, love, and enjoy God, and partake of the additional pleasures of Heaven as well as they who lived longer on earth. They, and they alone, enjoy the happiness of Heaven entirely as a free gift of God, without any cooperation of their own. They are in Heaven in virtue of their adoption as children of God and through the merits of Jesus Christ.

Whatever may be their degree of glory, we certainly can never place them on a level with the Apostles, martyrs, confessors, virgins, religious, and pious people who have fought a good fight against the world, the Devil, and the flesh. They never sinned, it is true, but neither did they ever make an act of faith, hope, or charity, or perform any other act of virtue. Hence, theirs may be called a crown of liberality, for they enjoy their beatitude as a free gift of God's unspeakable liberality. Their never-ending song is, therefore, one of gratitude to God for taking them out of the world before their souls could be defiled by sin, or their little hearts turned away from virtue by the fascinations of the world.

---

[126]Cf. St. Thomas Aquinas, *The Three Greatest Prayers* (Manchester, New Hampshire: Sophia Institute Press, 1990), 90.

The Happiness of Heaven

∞

All in Heaven are one family

Here, then, kind reader, we have the whole multitude that we saw standing around the throne of God. Although we have divided them into different classes and considered their glory separately, you must not infer that the blessed are really separated from each other in Heaven. For however greatly the glory of the highest may differ from that of the lowest, they all compose one great family of brothers and sisters, of whom God is the Father, Jesus Christ the elder Brother and the King, and Mary the Mother, as well as the Queen. They all mingle converse, and otherwise enjoy each other's society, for they are all united by the bond of the purest charity. They all exclaim with the royal prophet, "Behold, how good and how pleasant it is for brethren to dwell together in unity. . . . For there, the Lord hath commanded blessing, and life forevermore."[127]

They all are happy, because they all see, love, and enjoy God, as well as the additional pleasures with which He perfects and completes the happiness of His beloved children. They are all filled to overflowing with the happiness of which the royal prophet speaks when he says, "They shall be inebriated with the plenty of Thy house, and Thou shalt make them drink of the torrent of Thy pleasure. For with Thee is the fountain of life."[128] By their union with the Fountain of Life, which is God Himself, the blessed see all their desires fulfilled, and, knowing not what more to crave, they rest in God as their last end and enjoy Him forever.

[127]Ps. 132:1, 3 (RSV = Ps. 133:1, 3).
[128]Ps. 35:9-10 (RSV = Ps. 36:8-9).

∞

Chapter Sixteen

Your happiness will never end

Having endeavored, in the foregoing pages, to form for ourselves some idea of the glorious happiness reserved for us in Heaven, there still remains to say something of its crowning glory — the eternity of its duration. This is not only its crowning glory, but is, moreover, an essential constituent of that unspeakable joy which now inebriates the souls of the blessed. A moment's reflection will make this evident.

Let us suppose, for the sake of illustration, that on the last day, God should thus speak to the blessed: "Dearly beloved children, you are now happy, and you shall continue so for a very long time, but not forever. When I promised you eternal life, I did not really mean a life without end. I alone can live forever. I have created a little bird whose office it is, every thousand years, to take away from the earth one grain of sand, or a drop of water, and carry it to the place I have appointed. And when it will have thus removed the whole earth — all the oceans, rivers, and lakes — you shall all die a second death and be no more forever."

How many ages do you think it would take, at that rate, to remove this whole world to another place? Of course, you cannot even form a conception of the countless ages it would require. The most gifted mind is bewildered and lost in those millions and billions of ages. It seems as if that little bird never would come to the last atom, and to us, children of time, that vast duration seems like an eternity. And yet, if such a revelation were made to the blessed, they would again sorrow and mourn; the tears would again flow from their eyes, because the cankerworm that eats away all earthly happiness would have found entrance into Heaven.

Evidently, then, the eternity of Heaven is essential to complete the happiness of God's children.

Among the many defects which mar our happiness in this world, there are three capital ones, which we shall consider for a few moments. The happiness of this world is not and cannot be permanent, because we are changeable, because the objects of our happiness are also subject to change, and finally, because death must eventually tear us away from this world.

∞

Heaven will remove your fickleness

We ourselves are changeable by nature. This is a defect which must cling to us as long as we remain pilgrims here below. The objects which made us so happy in our childhood are no longer able to give us any pleasure. Our growth to mature age has completely changed us in their regard. Where is the man who could now spend the day with the playthings of his childhood? Where is the woman who could spend her time dressing and adorning a doll? We have changed, and other objects have become necessary.

But, in our mature years, we still continue to change, and those objects which make us happy today may, in a few days, be a source of annoyance to us, and even of wretchedness. The changes of the weather, our passions, our health, our associations, a want of success in our undertakings, an unkind word or look — all these, and a thousand other things, influence us and change our dispositions at times so completely that nothing in the whole world can make us feel happy. We are disgusted with everything that only yesterday made us as happy as we could expect to be in this world.

So great is our natural fickleness that we are continually exposed to change in regard to God, and thus lose the only happiness worth possessing — His friendship. For, after having, in all sincerity, promised and even sworn fidelity to Him, we may, at any moment, give way to our passions, and, like Peter, deny Him, or, like Judas, sell Him for a temporary gratification.

This fickleness, which so stubbornly clings to us in our present state of existence, and which puts an end to so many of our joys, is entirely removed by our union with God in the Beatific Vision. "We shall be like Him, because we shall see Him as He is." One of the essential attributes of God is immutability, or the total absence of change, or even of the power to change. He is the same forever. He is, as St. James beautifully expresses it, "The Father of lights, with whom there is no change nor shadow of alteration."[129] By our union with Him we are "made partakers of the divine nature" and, consequently, of the divine immutability. Our natural fickleness will die in our temporal death, never to rise again, and our whole nature will be clothed with immutability and remain the same forever.

[129]James 1:17.

Hence, we shall no longer be tossed to and fro by every wind of passion, nor by the vicissitudes of present time. We shall no longer, as now, be joyful one day and then be cast down and sorrowful the next; in the enjoyment of perfect health one day and racked with the pangs of disease on the next; enjoying the society of our fellow beings one day and finding it intolerable the next; overflowing now with devotion and the love of God and then ready to abandon His service in disgust. We shall become immutable, and therefore when millions of ages have rolled by, we shall still be enjoying the same happiness as we did when the vision of God first flashed upon our souls.

∞

In Heaven, sources of happiness will be immutable

But there is a second defect which, even if we were immutable ourselves, would prevent our earthly happiness from being permanent, and it is this: the objects from which we derive our happiness are also subject to change. Their beauty fades away. They lose their freshness and, along with it, the power of making us happy.

It was this defect which marred the happiness of Solomon. His position and circumstances placed within his reach all the pleasures which the heart of man can enjoy here below. He was a king, a husband, and a father; he was filled with a wisdom greater than ever was vouchsafed to any other man. He built temples and cities; he was visited by kings and queens, admired and almost worshiped as a god, on account of the magnificence with which he was surrounded; and yet he was not happy. But listen to his own confession, and ponder it well: "I heaped together for myself silver and gold, and the wealth of kings and provinces; . . . and I surpassed in riches all that were before me in Jerusalem; my wisdom also remained with me. And whatever my eyes desired, I refused them not; and I withheld not my heart from enjoying every pleasure, and delighting itself in all the things I had prepared. . . . And when I turned myself to all the works which my hands had wrought, and the labors wherein I had labored in vain, I saw in all things vanity, and vexation of mind, and that nothing was lasting under the sun."[130]

Here is the confession of one of the wisest of men — a man who tasted more of this world's happiness than any other; and he found it imperfect, and even vexatious, because "nothing was lasting under the sun."

But this is not all. Creatures not only change, fade away, and lose their power of giving us pleasure, but they may even turn against us and, after having been almost a heaven to us, become a very hell, by the afflictions and woes they bring upon us. This is especially the case if the object of our happiness is a human creature. Look at the dissensions and quarrels among friends and relatives who once loved each other so well. Look at the almost incredible number of divorces which take place nearly every day. They tell us that the happiness which comes to us from human creatures is not lasting, because man is mutable.

Take the virtuous and unfortunate Catherine of Aragon as an illustrious example. When King Henry VIII married her, he certainly made her happy at first, but as time rolled on, he

---

[130]Eccles. 2:8-11.

changed in her regard. His love grew cold; he gradually despised her, took away from her the title of queen, banished her from his presence, and married another woman! What a terrible reverse of fortune! He, who at first had been her joy, changed and became the cause of her deepest sorrow and wretchedness.

Oh, how differently shall we share in our heavenly home! For the objects of our love there are not mutable, as in this world. He who is the very source of our exceeding happiness is the eternal, immutable God. When He shall have united us to Himself, and made us "partakers of the divine nature," He never will change in our regard, tire of us, despise us, or cast us away from Him, as creatures do — no, never. The bare thought of such a misfortune would spread a shade of gloom on the bright faces of the blessed. Once we are united to Him in the Beatific Vision, He will love us forevermore. Never can there come a day when He will frown upon us and make us feel that His love for us has grown cold. Never will there come a day when His divine beauty will fade away, or when He will lose His power of making us happy, as is the case with the creatures that now surround us; and therefore we shall never see the day when our happiness will change, or cease to exist.

But there is still more. Not only is God immutable, and therefore unable to change in our regard, but all the companions of our bliss will have also become immutable in their love for us. Hence, there never will come a day when we shall see ourselves despised and even hated by our fellow creatures, as so often happens in this world. All those defects which now make us so unamiable will be totally removed by our union with God, and no one will ever see anything in us but what is good and deserving of love. From this it follows that even the happiness which comes to the blessed from creatures is permanent — eternal.

∞

Death has no place in Heaven

Let us now pass to the third defect of all earthly happiness. Even if both we and the objects which make us happy were immutable, our blessedness could not be lasting, because death, inexorable death, must eventually tear us away from them, or tear them away from us. All earthly happiness, glory, and greatness end in death. "And as it is appointed unto men once to die,"[131] it follows that all, both great and small, must eventually see the end of all that makes life bright and desirable according to nature. All must die, and no one can take along with him his glory or earthly happiness, for, as the Holy Spirit tells us, "Be thou not afraid, when a man shall be made rich, and when the glory of his house shall be increased. For when he shall die, he shall take nothing away; nor will his glory descend with him."[132]

Now where is the happiness and the glory of those mighty kings and queens who were once surrounded with all the magnificence of this world? The grave answers: "It is no more." Now where is the glory of those mighty conquerors who placed their supreme happiness in subjugating nations to their way, in making widows and orphans, and in spreading

[131]Heb. 9:27.
[132]Ps. 48:17-18 (RSV = Ps. 49:16-17).

devastation and ruin wherever they went? It is no more! We can say of them, in the words of the royal prophet, "I have seen the wicked highly exalted, and lifted up like the cedars of Libanus. And I passed by, and lo! he was not; and I sought him, and his place was not found."[133] Death laid its cold hand upon them and put an end to their earthly happiness.

In Heaven, that awful death shall be no more. We have the word of the living God for it: "And God shall wipe away all tears from their eyes; and death shall be no more, nor mourning, nor crying, nor sorrow shall be anymore, for the former things are passed away."[134] In very deed, "the former things have passed away" — sorrow, mourning, poverty, labor, the vicissitudes of time, temptations to sin — all of these things have passed away, never to return. The children of God have entered into the enjoyment of their inheritance, which shall never be torn away from them, because "death shall be no more."

Nevermore shall they see the dawn of a day when father and mother have to bid farewell — a long and sad farewell — to their heartbroken children, because "death shall be no more." Nevermore will there come a day upon which affectionate children have to imprint the last kiss upon the cold and pallid cheek of their dying parents, because "death shall be no more." Nevermore shall we see our kindred and friends slowly descending into the grave, nor hear the cold and cruel clods of earth falling upon them, because "death shall be no more."

[133]Ps. 36:35-36 (RSV = Ps. 37:35-36).
[134]Rev. 21:4.

"Death is swallowed up in victory. O death, where is thy victory? O death, where is thy sting?"[135] This is the joyful song of triumph which forever resounds through the vaults of Heaven, because "The just shall live forevermore, and their reward is with the Lord, and the care of them with the Most High. Therefore shall they receive a kingdom of glory, and a crown of beauty at the hand of the Lord."[136]

∞

Strive now for the happiness of Heaven

In conclusion, let me exhort you, Christian soul, to meditate often and seriously on the happiness of Heaven. Such meditations, besides deepening our knowledge of God and of the things He has prepared for those who love Him, have a wonderful power of detaching our hearts from the transitory pleasures and honors of this world. Moreover, they create in our soul an unquenchable thirst for the vision and possession of God, while they infuse into us a new courage to battle manfully against all the obstacles which beset our path in the practice of virtue.

Such meditations fill us, moreover, with a laudable and noble ambition of reaching a high degree of union with God. This was the ambition of the saints, and it should be ours also. It was this desire of a most intimate union with God that caused them to deny themselves even the most innocent pleasures of this world and to undergo sufferings, the bare recital of which makes our poor nature shudder. They knew that "our

[135] 1 Cor. 15:54-55.
[136] Wisd. 5:16-17.

present tribulation, which is momentary and light, worketh for us above measure exceedingly an eternal weight of glory."[137] Their meditations on eternal truths had convinced them "that the sufferings of this present time are not worthy to be compared with the glory to come, that shall be revealed in us."[138]

In the thirty-seventh chapter of her autobiography, St. Teresa speaks thus: "I would not lose, through any fault of mine, the least degree of further enjoyment. I even go so far as to declare that, if the choice were offered to me, whether I would rather remain subject to all the afflictions of the world, even to the end of it, and then ascend, by that means, to the possession of a little more glory in Heaven; or else, without any affliction at all, enjoy a little less glory, I would most willingly accept all of the troubles and afflictions for a little more enjoyment, so that I might understand a little more of the greatness of God; because I see that he who understands more of Him loves and praises Him so much the more." Here is the ambition of a great saint. It is not after crowns or scepters, or the glory of this world that she sighs, but after a single degree of higher enjoyment in Heaven; and to obtain that, she is willing to remain suffering in this wretched world until the end of time.

Let such be your ambition in the future. If not in so sublime a degree, let it, at least, be directed only to the acquisition of "treasures in Heaven, where neither moth nor rust consume, and where thieves do not break through and steal."[139] Labor

[137] 2 Cor. 4:17.
[138] Rom. 8:18.
[139] Matt. 6:19.

incessantly for that "inheritance incorruptible, undefiled, that cannot fade, reserved in Heaven for you."[140] "Be faithful until death," says our Lord Jesus Christ, "and I will give thee the crown of life."[141]

[140]1 Pet. 1:4.
[141]Rev. 2:10.

∞

Sophia Institute Press®